HEALING FOR THE WOUNDED LIFE

Healing for the Wounded Life

How to Understand Your Illness and Find Biblical Solutions

DR JOHN GORDON

THANKFUL BOOKS

Copyright © John Gordon 2007

First published 2007

Published by Thankful Books
c/o P.O. Box 2118, Seaford BN25 9AR,
in association with Philadelphia Books
P.O. Box 769, Lancaster LA1 9BF.

ISBN-13:   978 1 905084 10 4
ISBN-10:   1 905084 10 2

Unless otherwise indicated, biblical quotations are
from the New International Version © 1973, 1978, 1984
by the International Bible Society.

Book design and production for the publisher by
Bookprint Creative Services, <www.bookprint.co.uk>
Printed in Great Britain.

For the future generation
(as in Psalm 102:18)

CONTENTS

Acknowledgements 9
Preface 11

1. Introduction 13
2. Spirit, Soul and Body 27
3. Heart 46
4. Mind 62
5. Emotion 83
6. Sex 104
7. Human Nature 123
8. Community 143
9. Reality 163
10. Illness 185
11. Madness 204
12. Healing 225

Postscript 245
Prayers 248
Selected Bibliography 251

ACKNOWLEDGEMENTS

I acknowledge with respect and gratitude the help of Doctors H.A. Crawford, R.D. Laing and L. Redler years ago when these concepts were being formed in my mind.

I acknowledge most thankfully the wisdom and encouragement of Jack Hardwidge, when we lived in Exeter.

I thank the Reverend Doctor C.G. Bristow for having read the manuscript and for his helpful suggestions.

I have been especially blessed through the wisdom, faithful patience and many insights of my wife, Pamela.

PREFACE

We are spiritual beings with bodies. Relationships are spiritual influences that are constantly affecting each soul and living body. We are separate neither from our living, physical bodies nor from each other.

Our human nature changes when we meet Jesus and receive Him into the heart, physically committing ourselves to Him. The Bible says (John 6:63) "The Spirit gives life; the flesh counts for nothing." Healing of the spirit and soul, and sometimes of the physical body too, can come, by the grace of God, through allowing His Spirit to reconcile all our relationships, past and present, to God through Jesus. The Holy Spirit brings peace to the soul so that to be rightly related to God in loving community with others may eventually become as natural as breathing.

For the process of repentance to be adequate to allow God to change us into the people He desires, it is necessary to become aware of aspects of our human nature that are commonly camouflaged by science and humanism.

However, there is no need to oppose those who regard only in a physical way the subjects raised in this book. Technological medicine is invaluable for the treatment of emergencies and the management of established disease, and charitable help of a practical nature may patch us up and temporarily relieve distress.

Nevertheless, Christian spiritual healing can be significantly complementary and may reduce reliance on medical technology by eradicating the root of trouble.

CHAPTER ONE

INTRODUCTION

The gaunt remains of an old lunatic asylum impose a haunting unease just outside the city where I am living. Next door lies a large prison. Nearby rises the moor where criminals sentenced to death at the assizes used to be hanged.

Whilst the old mental hospital remains standing it serves as an unavoidable monument to thousands of people judged too strange, too difficult or too challenging to be included within civilised society, rejected, often hopeless and deprived of the means of salvation.

About a quarter of their number at any given time would seriously have accepted personal help for change of heart and healing if ever it had been offered and available[1]. But very few people working in such forlorn institutions ever had sufficient openness of mind and courage to attend faithfully to the disturbing truth of the experiences of those individuals. Jesus suffered for them outside the city gate to make them holy through His own blood (Hebrews 13:12). But churches tacitly imposed exclusive conditions of respectability on their approach to Jesus (see Romans 2:1).

---

[1] This is a rough calculation I once made when I was working in such a place.

This old psychiatric hospital, like so many others, is due for demolition. Soon there will be no obvious reminder of the gross human wretchedness that used to be confined within its walls. Its function has been taken over by selectively sedative drugs and subtly persuasive psychology, by suppression of madness and sickness rather than true healing. Although the wretchedness nevertheless remains – it is seen in every accident and emergency department, every police station, every doctor's consulting room and every social worker's case file – it is now disguised, made more respectable and less obvious. New drugs and humanistic psychology, backed up by television and popular magazines, make it easier to avoid its reality.

When a person's condition or demeanour seems unable adequately to be accounted for or explained in ordinary, non-technical terms, people commonly describe that person as ill. They say, "There must be something wrong with him!" However, if the condition or demeanour can easily be accounted for in terms that everyone can understand without much further enquiry, that person is accepted as being normal and responsible.

Then those deemed ill are given special treatment "outside the city gate", as it were, with permission through sick notes to be off work; or in hospital, if hospital technology is reckoned necessary. And those deemed responsible for serious offences are punished, and to some degree condemned, so that they may be seen to be abnormal and irresponsible. They are put in prison or put on probation or in some other way are put "outside the city gate". The reality of both illness and criminality tend to make a person different and tend to some extent to exclude a person from ordinary, normally responsible society. So quick fixes are popular.

The common presumption is that whatever malevolent influence is at work should always be able to be understood and fixed by human ingenuity and science. So the management of these human conditions is left to specialists, few of whom are Christian.

God is rarely consulted about illness or about habitual offending, except by presuming that in a nominally Christian society His laws should be able to be obeyed through good training and will-power. Not often do we ask God to reveal and heal the deeper issues, or the true meaning, so that souls may be healed. So His words usually fail to be incorporated into character and personality and fail to change society much. This way they only influence society's conscience. Thus the guilt and shame is increased without offering real healing. Guilt and shame breed rebellion and trouble and, whilst the godly relevance of illness and criminality are put out of sight and out of mind through being effectively suppressed by the humanistic application of science, many find it easy to live with the illusion that no one need ask God about them.

The lack of personal Christian understanding of the true spiritual nature of illness and criminality, and also of the nature of common malevolence and harm, is demonstrated by the failure of churches to engage with these issues, other than philanthropically though a form of charity which often lacks empathy.

Christian culture has been seduced into degeneracy by having been led into placing too much confidence in the highest impulses of human nature, by believing that moral self-determination lies within the autonomous power of human beings through their reason, and by denying the supernatural effect of the Holy Spirit through the word of God. As the church has failed to take hold of our most serious existential issues, allowing scientists and philosophers to deal with them and usually failing to respond in the power of the Spirit according to God's word, it has lost credibility. The experience of the poor and meek could have been grist to the mill to build the kingdom of God in His strength. The incidence of illness and madness would have been reduced if the light of Jesus had really been shed into the dark places of our individual and collective lives.

There has been a price to pay for the apparent progress of western Christian civilisation. The casualties of modernisation have been lives lost to war, disease, madness and famine (Revelation 6). Now we have the delusion of unreality as the appearance of suffering is removed from consciousness by technology (see 2 Thessalonians 2:9–15). But the oppressiveness of the delusion only becomes apparent to those who seek the face of God in their suffering, and they are put "outside the city gate" and their evidence is thereby discounted. "The heart of the wise is in the house of mourning, but the heart of fools is in the house of pleasure" (Ecclesiates 7:4).

As western Christian culture has naturally degenerated a culture of immediate gratification of wants has become increasingly sophisticated through science backed up by humanist philosophy. Priority is given to symptom relief and convenience. Little thought is given to the spiritual meaning of illness and evil or to what God may be saying and doing. Clever new remedies are reckoned good and the nature of wisdom is disputed. As the authority of God the Father is effectively called into question, so all other authority is impugned and the sense of duty disappears. People are treated impersonally as if they were machines and care is sold as a commodity, like prostitution. Scientific technology is expected to control sickness so that we can do what we want when we want and keep working.

In contrast, God works personally. Everything has meaning as part of His universe. We ignore His meaning at our peril.

So any modern physician attending the sick who is truly Christian cannot serve both God and mammon, and must therefore study to be shrewd but innocent both in the use of the technology available and in personal relationships. Although science may offer symptom relief, the resolution of spiritual issues may prove more worthwhile although it can sometimes be complex, unpaid and time-consuming. Spiritual issues can always be found in sickness. Addressing them may involve some opposition to the popular culture, some suffering, some acknowledgement of human failing and some perseverance, some costly personal change (not least in the attendants) all of which may require some guidance.

If a person desires to move beyond mere symptom relief into healing Godly wisdom, rather than technological expertise, is necessary. Healing usually involves paying attention to very personal matters that are revealed as the Holy Spirit is allowed to shed His light into dark areas of the soul. It involves getting them right with God. It often becomes necessary to accept real care from other people whose authority you trust. Thus healing involves personal relationships. Sadly, however, words and appearances can be so deceptive that it can often be very difficult to know whom to trust. Furthermore, swimming against the tide of the culture we live in can be hard.

All wounds tend to heal naturally, however, and healing may be greatly assisted by appropriate care and symptom relief. This is the proper place of medical technology. Nevertheless, things may still keep on going wrong, and illness may recur. In order to stop becoming ill personal change may be necessary. There is a dimension to healing that involves freeing the soul from deceptive spiritual influences, from wounds and from sin; a wise physician guides a person towards it, although to be forced towards it will always be counter-productive. This path of life is narrow (Matthew 7:14).

Cure and healing

Cure is promoted by care: putting a dressing on a wound, making the invalid comfortable, offering the medicine and help that will alleviate the distress. Care accepts the sickness, the mess and disability and eases the symptoms. Real care is given personally, with generosity, compassion, love, truth. It makes you feel better and encourages the natural healing processes that are innate in God's creation. So it changes your outlook and makes your wounds less grievous so that the repercussions are not so bad as they might otherwise have been. If the real issues are truthfully addressed and God's wisdom is sought you find yourself moving along your way, away from death. Good care encourages natural healing.

Healing by divine command may seem rather different because it has a more immediately supernatural dimension. When you are healed in this way the sickness obeys the command until it has gone. Sometimes the healing is immediate and sometimes it is a process that takes time. This sort of healing is miraculous, a demonstration of the authoritative hand of God against the apparent odds.

Jesus' parable about the good Samaritan (Luke 10:25–37) is about care. The Samaritan took pity on a man who had been severely injured and robbed. He helped his wounds to heal by washing them with oil and wine, and then by bandaging them, and he took him to an inn where he paid the innkeeper to look after him for a while. Jesus said to his hearers: "Go and do likewise!" However, when Jesus told this story the big surprise for his listeners was that the Samaritan was the natural enemy of the injured man. This way Jesus taught His followers to love not only their neighbours but also even their enemies so that they may find healing. Jesus' disciples are enabled to do this through the gift of the Holy Spirit. This sort of care is a distinctly Christian gift. It becomes possible to hate the sin but to love the sinner and to care for people without necessarily approving of their actions or beliefs.

Although most professional care-givers these days aspire to work in this way, namely with disinterested compassion, the resources necessary to continue to do so are spiritual and distinctly Christian. People have always sought divine healing from their gods but the nature of that healing and the quality of the compassion has differed accordingly. The hospitals and welfare agencies where disciplined, careful and tolerant hospitality dramatically improved the healing of the afflicted and poor were initially developed throughout the world by the out-working of practical Christianity.

If the necessary spiritual resources are not to disappear from among us by neglect, the continuance of the legacy of disinterested care depends on the continuance of public Christian worship in spirit and truth and on continued Christian awareness that no individual is beyond redemption.

In Europe, Christian worship has been increasingly compromised by trying to placate the secular world, and the organisation of care for the sick has nowadays mostly become humanistic. As the Christian heritage is being allowed to decay, so the impoverishment of spiritual resources is subtly failing to sustain a good enough quality of care. Children are killed – aborted from the womb – in large numbers. Old people are often not treated with personal dignity. Serious consideration is given to eugenics. Spiritual distress is given a psychiatric label and suppressed with medication instead of being addressed truthfully. And litigation against the medical profession is increasingly common because people often do not feel truly cared about or understood.

It is, after all, not natural for us to love other people who offend and distress us. Only those who personally know Jesus' divine forgiveness, and what He accomplished on the cross, have the capacity entirely to overcome their natural tendency to retaliate. Although it may be disguised, the common attitude amongst people who do not have the Holy Spirit is that when people are nasty they should be treated in a nasty way in return. This leads to an escalation of trouble as bad reaction naturally begets bad reaction, which may become habitual. Secular care that is essentially scientific and humanistic can be expected to evolve according to its nature so as to become mechanistic and utilitarian, which will eventually cause widespread dismay and dissatisfaction because people who are ill want personal kindness and hope beyond what is reasonable.

The supernatural dimension of love and care is not the only healing blessing found amongst followers of Jesus. When people came to the Lord Jesus for healing, illnesses left them at His touch or rebuke. He also drove out their demons. Although this sort of healing is often called miraculous, the Holy Spirit has always worked in this way, against the apparent odds, through prophets and saints. Jesus gives His disciples the authority to do the same as He did (Matthew 10:1 and 28:18–20). Jesus says that where two or three come together into His name He is there with them (Matthew 18:20) and the word of God says that if any believer is sick the elders of the church should be called together to pray over the sick person and anoint the sick person with oil and the Lord will heal that person (James 5:15). He has healed me like this, with the help of His present-day elders, and healing like this may be expected when sick people turn to Jesus. When faith comes for the healing there will be a moment in His presence when the sickness may authoritatively be driven away.

However, Jesus said: "no one can come to me unless the Father has enabled him" (John 8:65). So the enabling work of the Father will have been going on in people, often without their being aware of it, before they seriously come to Jesus for His authoritative help. It follows that there is a time and a place for miracles of healing and they should not be expected to happen just because they seem to be a good idea. The Father's changes have to be working inside a person for the faith to develop.

The two sorts of healing, both godly Christian care and miraculous healing with authority in His name, are commanded by our Lord Jesus. Those who are wounded, in whatever way, are to be tended with mercy and dispassionate love, cared for individually and cured, and whenever the faith is present they should seek Jesus' authority to dispel whatever besets them.

Healing is most promising when the natural healing processes innate in the body are enabled to function most efficiently. This will be found in a milieu where God's presence is unimpeded, where people are rightly related both to Him and to each other according to His word. There it will be possible to receive His words so that the root cause of the sickness may be expelled in the name of Jesus. God's love and God's words ministered personally through disinterested compassion bring peace to the soul and to the body with a supernatural dimension which can never be matched by any scientific treatment programme. When the sick person is in God's hands, listening obediently to His voice, that person need not waste energy with the stress of fighting for self-preservation.

It follows that the best sort of care will be given by people with the Holy Spirit in them. Since secular resources are limited, it is time for the business of healing to be reclaimed by the Christian church. Christians should add their dimension, for those who want it, to the work of the secular agencies. The purpose of this book is to help develop a better understanding of this Christian spiritual dimension.

Technological care

These days, oil and wine have been superseded not only by much stronger antiseptics but also by drugs which can be ingested in order to control the disease process. Care has become very technological. Modern remedies and treatments are often life-saving so if someone gets pneumonia, for example, the penicillin may stop the disease in a way that seems miraculous.

Some of us remember the days before antibiotics, when you could not be at all sure whether someone with a bad case of pneumonia would live or die. The crisis could be extremely distressing. Probably more people prayed more in those days.

Penicillin and all the other modern drugs, and medical and surgical technology, have taken away a lot of the old anxieties and they have given people much more confidence and hope for when they are ill. Since the technology can be trusted there may seem to be no need for faith in God.

We should understand clearly, however, that modern scientific medical treatments are about cure, rather than about authoritative miracles in the name of Jesus. If we look at what penicillin actually does we find that it kills the bacteria which have infested the lungs. After it has been given to someone with a pneumonia that is susceptible to it, the natural healing processes with which God has graciously endued the living body become much more efficient in healing the tissues. But the healing actually takes place in just the same way that the man set upon by thieves in Jesus' parable found his healing as he was tended and rested at the inn.

A famous sixteenth-century physician, Ambroise Paré, is credited with having said "I tend them, God heals them". Godly physicians will still say the same today. However sophisticated the modern medical technology may be, it remains a means of tending whilst God heals. Surgery may remove the tumour, insulin may cure the diabetes, a painkiller may stop the headache and penicillin may kill the pathogen, but strictly speaking none of these remedies is healing in itself. Rather, good medical treatment arrests the disease process and helps natural healing to proceed by God's grace with maximum efficiency and minimum complication. Sometimes, too, it makes good the damage artificially, as when insulin is given to replace that which can no longer be made in the body.

Sir Robert Hutchinson's prayer influenced several generations of British physicians: "From inability to leave well alone, from too much zeal for what is new and contempt for what is old, from putting knowledge before wisdom, service before art, cleverness before common sense, from treating patients as cases and from making the care of a disease more grievous than its endurance Good Lord deliver us."

The quality of professional attendance epitomized in this prayer gained general respect. It was personal but professional and it left room for the wisdom of God.

Meaning

A question not asked often enough is why this particular illness should afflict this particular person at this particular time in this particular place. These days, when there is a pill for every ill, we tend to consider such enquiries irrelevant. Furthermore, if these questions are indeed asked we tend to be satisfied with mechanistic answers. We say "He got wet and cold and developed pneumonia," but we do not ask, "What was going on for him to get wet and cold in the first place, and to have such poor resistance to infection, and why were his lungs attacked?"

The word of God says the very hairs of our heads are all numbered (Matthew 10:30) and therefore, since God knows and loves us so intimately, every illness we suffer must be known to God and must have meaning. Although we may, in fact, occasionally ask the doctor why we are ill, too often we do not ask God, although it would be appropriate to do so every time. We should then ask God for His remedies and instructions, as He does not want us to be ill (see Exodus 15:26).

When God speaks to us about the meaning of what we may be suffering He does not usually say, "You should not have gone out in the wet and cold." He is far more likely to say something like "I have been trying to tell you for a long time that you need not be so dispirited but now that you are forced by your physical condition to rest perhaps you will take heart when I tell you to repent of fighting battles which I have not asked you to fight and allow me to surprise you with what I really want you to do for me so that I may heal your lungs and inspire you afresh."

God does not use the reasonable, abstract, mechanistic language of this technological world. He speaks to the heart rather than the mind; gently through revelation, personally, intimately and persistently. The meaning of whatever we are suffering becomes apparent if we are open to hearing it and if we develop and continue a real personal relationship with Him through

Jesus (John 14:6) bringing our anxieties to Him (1 Peter 5:6–7) and holding nothing back from Him. When we receive His words to us, in repentance and faith, and then live them in our lives for real, we change. Thus His command to be healed becomes effective.

God knows everything and knows our hearts (1 John 3:20). He is in charge and is working His purposes out (Psalm 33, Jeremiah 32:19, etc.). For God everything has meaning. Although we cannot fully fathom the mind of the Lord, those who belong to Him have the mind of Christ and God does reveal His thoughts to us (1 Corinthians 2:16, Amos 3:7, 4:13, etc.). In fact He has told us that "there is nothing hidden that will not be disclosed, and nothing concealed that will not be known or brought out into the open" (Luke 8:17). It therefore follows that everything that happens to us is known to God and has meaning, which He may allow us to know in order that we may move closer to Him through repentance.

Furthermore, He does not show us the meaning of our sicknesses in order to feed our intellectual pride, or so that we should make better rules for living, but rather so that we should let go of our human reckonings and grow to trust Him more and know Him better. Changes are incorporated through the healing activity of His Spirit in us when we are humble enough before Him to allow Him to work in us. He does not force us or tell us everything He is doing. Although we may not be particularly aware of having learned any lesson by being reconciled to God, we shall have moved on along the path of life. God's meaning becomes apparent in our changed lives. We change by becoming more like Him. So He is revealed.

The word of God tells us that those who find God's healing are those who listen carefully to His voice and consequently who obey what is right in His eyes (Exodus 15:26). God also tells us that when people do not include Him in what they do, and do not stay right with Him, the devil may find a legitimate right to bring upon them and upon their descendants one or more of the curses, wounds and sicknesses described in Deuteronomy Chapter 28.

Furthermore, we are told that God disciplines those He loves. Those who listen to the Lord Jesus and follow Him as disciples learn obedience through what they suffer in this world, and they gain His peace by His healing (Deuteronomy 8:5, Hebrews 12:1–14). He tells us He will always provide a way out and will not send us more than we can bear (1 Corinthians 10:13). So as well as exposing us to the temptations of the world and of the flesh God may also allow the devil some access to our lives, as He did with Job (Job 1:8), so that we may grow closer to Him as we endure, persevere and overcome through His Spirit. This process is not pleasant although we may in fact know His joy in our suffering (James 1:2). And nothing in the word of God indicates that physical or mental illness may not be included in what we suffer in this way.

Salvation may be found in repentance and rest (Isaiah 30:15) and during the process the meaning of our illness may be uncovered. As we become more fully reconciled to God (Colossians 1:22, Romans 8:11) miracles of healing may be expected when the faith comes.

Full personal healing does not always happen, although it always remains possible. Distress and suffering will not be removed from this fallen world until there is a new heaven and a new earth (Revelation 21:1–4). Meanwhile we suffer difficulties and deformities, wretchedness and wounds that we can use to learn obedience and purify our souls. Our sufferings and our illnesses always have meaning for God. Although He loves us as we are, He tirelessly pursues His purpose, in all its complexity, to restore us to dwell with Him in the individual place He has for each one. So it behoves us to clear away as best we may whatever gets in the way of hearing Him.

Our sins and everything we would prefer to hide are known to Him, and He knows their meaning. Healing comes from being open and truthful and real with God, and with one another, and allowing ourselves to change in order to become more like God, which is possible when we know Jesus. Knowing the meaning of what we suffer may help us to find healing by revealing how to repent and accept God's changes. No sin is beyond redemption except, of course, the sin of refusing Him (Matthew 12:31). Who we are, and how we are, has significance for Him and He loves us jealously. The parts of our bodies have meaning for Him (Romans 6:13). All the things He has created have meaning for Him (Psalms 33:13–15, 147:4–5 etc.). He wants us to use His creation in accordance with the covenants He has made with mankind and with His instructions. So in trying to describe our human nature and experience in these terms it is necessary to shed the light of God into dark places where His meaning has been hidden (Ephesians 5:8–14).

CHAPTER TWO

SPIRIT, SOUL AND BODY

Our spiritual nature

Genesis 1 and Psalm 8 record that God made human beings to
rule in this world. He created us to be rulers over the works of
His hands and He put everything under our feet.

Sadly, our human race lost intimacy with God through being
deceived by Satan. So we have mostly failed to use our God-
given abilities for our creator. In general we have not lived in
harmony with God nor done what He has been doing. Instead
we have used our authority, powers and talents to analyse
everything God has created in order to use our knowledge to
manipulate and dominate our environment for our own ends,
according to what we think is good, and according to our own
human agenda. Our own collective reasoning about good and
evil conflicts with the mind of God as revealed through holy
Scripture (note Genesis 2:17).

We become so busy in our efforts to manage without God
that we fail to see that we are spiritual beings made by God in
His own image and made to live in personal relationship with
Him. Despite having fallen from a state of grace our relationships and personalities are spiritual and, whether we like it or

27

not and whether we are conscious of it or not, other spiritual beings influence our lives.

I have no doubt about the existence of demons and angels and of principalities and authorities in spiritual realms, all of whom are spiritual people who are not usually seen in physical bodies in this world but with whom it is nevertheless possible for human beings to have some relationship. I shall refer to them in accordance with the Holy Bible. Although my concern is to see our own human condition and our spiritual nature in God's way (Colossians 2:13–15), it is not my purpose to concern myself unduly with the unseen world or to write any sort of demonology or angelology.

On the face of things many people commonly insist that the spiritual world does not exist, although secretly most people would accept that it does. This contradiction exists because to admit the reality of the spiritual world would mean admitting that we people are not really in control. Therefore it would involve acknowledging the power of God. So most people say belief in the supernatural is irrational and they relegate spiritual considerations to superstition and occultism, and treat spiritual matters as if they were unreal. This way they can avoid taking account of God in their everyday lives.

Sigmund Freud, the founder of psychoanalysis, argued that our sexuality was the subject of the greatest taboos and the cause of so much personal conflict, repression and illness. However, I believe he was really speaking about much more than sexuality and was essentially considering the creative spiritual power by which we seem to be lived and to whom we are accountable. In their attempt to be scientific and academically credible, and despite extensive Jewish influence, he and his followers interpreted their discoveries without solemn reference to the God of Abraham, Isaac and Jacob. It is the truthful knowledge of the presence of this creator God and the consequent awareness of the spiritual nature of our fall away from Him that is the great taboo for so many human beings.

A particular trouble is that when God is known through Jesus sin is seen in its true perspective. Not only sexual abuses but also every other sort of abuse of the fact that we were made in the image of God, and every sort of bondage in which we become trapped as a result, become apparent in His light. Suddenly the world is not such a nice place. This is altogether too much to consider for many people. Sin and shame are far too much to bear if you have no escape, no hope of divine mercy and love. People essentially retain some sense of condemnation until they know about Jesus' atonement. There is no hope of healing and no relief until they know that God grants repentance and comfort and healing to those who will accept Jesus.

The liberation of the personal human libido, which Freud powerfully facilitated, has released many once-private difficulties into the social and political domain. Freud helped us to bring them to light, and there seems no doubt that his Jewish heritage helped him to do so, but he did not have the power to set us free. So-called sexual freedoms have contributed to the breakdown of the family, and to a liberal tolerance of doing what you want, which have undermined the social structures that once provided stability. Unless the authority of Jesus is brought into individual lives, the liberation of people to do what they want ultimately results in terror. The terror and panic are the same whether they are produced by Dionysiac revels or whether they are the result of holocaust. Having lost all defensiveness and resistance, a person faces existing in death. The power to be free is not political or social, and it is not within the control of human beings. It is spiritual and it only comes from Almighty God.

Analysis may elucidate hidden issues, and technology may help us to be cared for, but true healing is found through personal spiritual relationship with God. If we fail to keep a check on the extent to which we invest our faith in scientific analysis and technology we may fail to leave room for God.

The Holy Bible says the only way to come into relationship with God without being deceived is through His only begotten Son, the Lord Jesus Christ of Nazareth (John 14:6), God made human, who went through death by crucifixion and overcame it in order to save us from our sin and from the power of Satan, and who rose victorious from the dead the third day afterwards. All gods want people's lives but no other god has ever gone through death to save people; other gods take people's lives into death. Through personally accepting Jesus there comes His authority to overcome our fallen nature and to overcome death, to be free and to know His peace.

You may meet the Lord Jesus Christ of Nazareth by calling to Him by name. Or you may be introduced to Him by someone else. If you are seeking Him, wittingly or unwittingly, one way or another He will reveal Himself to you. Although you will probably not actually see Him in the flesh you will know His presence. Then you can get to know Him more and more. He has the power to enable you to overcome the demon of death and all the other demons. Through His Spirit, which He will impart, you will find yourself worshipping Him, repenting of your sin, accepting His forgiveness, forgiving other people who have hurt you and making Him Lord in your heart for everything you do in your life. Your spirit comes alive and the power to overcome the pull of death changes your personality. His presence with you brings a completeness and peace which your spirit, soul and body receive gladly and never want to relinquish.

His Spirit becomes sealed into your heart, at some moment when your heart is yielded to Him, so that He does not go away (Ephesians 1:13). This means baptism in Holy Spirit (Matthew 3:11, Acts 2) through which you will find your tongue loosened so that you may speak with Him in your own spiritual language. Then the key to allowing Him to change every part of you, spirit, soul and body, is to present your living body to Him all the time, to belong to Him totally, so that what you do will always be under His authority, in His service and for His glory (Romans 12:1).

The prayer at the end of the book may help. Churches would be much more interesting places if all that pertains to this sort of thing were grist to the mill of their everyday conversation.

These words printed in ink on these paper pages carry a living spiritual message that can change your life. Similarly, the lifeless material world that is so avidly analysed and studied by science is ineffably transcended by the spiritual world of living relationships. The signs of our spiritual nature are really quite obvious to those who have eyes to see them.

The God who created us is the God of Abraham, Isaac and Jacob, and He is the One who ardently desires both our worship and a close relationship with us, so that we walk His way with Him. Only when we accept and join with His Son Jesus, however, may we know him closely as Father. Through Jesus He adopts us into His family and brings us into the kingdom of eternal life.

The Holy Spirit jealously restrains those who love Him from intimacy with anyone else they may fancy, seen or unseen. So if we love Him we shall allow Him to regulate our relationships.

When somebody dies

Many people avoid open intellectual consideration of the spiritual world due to their hidden fear of death. The removal from our everyday awareness of the experience of people dying serves to exacerbate this fear. Sadly, old folk often do not live and die with the rest of us because going to work makes us too frenetic to care for them and we usually feel constrained to put all illness entirely into the technological hands of professionals who must legally do all they can to keep us going and keep a person alive. We have forgotten that there is a time to die. We have forgotten how to care for the dying because we have forgotten how to die well.

It can be hard to think about death. Many people despair that they can see no way to have their family around them at peace when they die and many people are frightened that all sorts of difficult things may have to happen to them before they are allowed to pass away. The people around us may not have a faith strong enough to overcome their fear of it. They may never have figured out for themselves how to handle dying. Few people dare to acknowledge that death is not the end but that after death we shall all be resurrected in the flesh (1 Corinthians 15) and will inevitably have to give an account of ourselves to God. To die well is to be prepared for this and to die amongst others who themselves are so prepared.

The word of God says that when we die we shall leave our bodies and either go to live with God or go to be with the souls of the dead and that sooner or later all people will be resurrected in their bodies to give an account to God and receive His judgement (see Revelation 20). In order to avoid eternal torment and have our names written in God's book of life, we need to belong with Him so that as we mature in this world we change to become more like Him. In Hebrews 12:14 it says that without holiness no one will see the Lord. This means that if we have a relationship with God, through Jesus, His Spirit can sort us out, if we let Him, before we die so that we can be reconciled to God and give a good account of ourselves and have an eternal place with Him amongst the living.

The prayer of Paul recorded in 1 Thessalonians 5:23 bears witness that this God of peace is able to sanctify us completely in spirit, soul and body so that we may appear before Him blameless. This speaks of every part of us being transformed by the Spirit of God, including the various parts of our physical bodies, and our hearts, minds, emotions and relationships. In reality, this involves walking humbly with God in repentance and healing as we grow closer to God. We become able to face death with equanimity when the Holy Spirit living in us gives us an assurance of salvation, a real hope of having being reconciled and made all right with God (see Colossians 1:21–23) despite our imperfections.

When you are with someone who is in the process of passing out of this world and ceasing to inhabit their body the distinctions between spirit, soul and body make more sense.

Often the people who are close to someone dying will have become aware that the spirit of that person is ebbing. Sooner or later there comes a moment when the breathing stops, the heart no longer beats and the blood no longer circulates. The body is suddenly no longer inhabited by that spiritual personality. The soul has gone and only a lifeless corpse remains.

Thereafter the corpse begins to decompose. Whether buried or cremated it will sooner or later become part of the soil. The elements of the earth from which the actual body has been formed return to the earth, ashes to ashes, dust to dust (as written in *The Book of Common Prayer*).

Personality

The process of dying is the reverse of the process of creation as described in Genesis 2:7 which tells how God formed mankind from the dust of the ground and breathed the breath of life into the nostrils to create a living soul. Elements of the earth are spiritually united in a living organism. A soul with unique personality and singular talents and qualities is given at conception. Through the spirit, a body becomes individually alive and that living principle, the soul, is responsive to other animate beings and capable of maturing in complex sentient reciprocity with them. Each human body, too, has qualities which distinguish it from any other human body.

Functions and qualities are not only differentiated within the parts of the individual body but also both within and between social groups of people (1 Corinthians 12:12–31). God knew each person, spirit, soul and body, before we came into being in this world (see Psalm 139) and placed each one of us in different families, communities and nations.

All the living activity of the person, spiritual, social and physical, reveals the personality. Personality is a spiritual entity made manifest in this world through relationships both with other personalities and with things. Personalities have influence in this world through their relationships. They change the world. Through the complexity of all that is going on in our various changing relationships we live in a state of perpetual change, whether we are aware of the fact or not. We change and the world changes and in fact God is in charge of the process. He holds it all together.

Through the vicissitudes of living in our bodies in this fallen world our character changes and circumstances change. Rebellion against Him can only lead to trouble sooner or later. If we refuse to allow God to change us in His way, and refuse to do what God is doing, we may change so as to become ill. The dynamics of God's life in us may implode, as it were, and go bad.

If we have given our bodies to Him and constantly accept that Jesus shed His blood on the cross to save us, we may refer to Him in all our relationships, and in all the joys and troubles that beset us. He enables us to become more like Himself (2 Corinthians 3:18) and to find abundant and eternal life through our particular part in doing what He is doing. We may constantly wash ourselves clean of this fallen, selfish, human world, and of our natural reactions to it, by receiving His word into our hearts. We shall know His direction, and His power to overcome, through His presence with us.

Because this fallen world is difficult and painful, our pilgrimage with God involves suffering. Scripture records that Jesus learned obedience in this world through what He suffered and it is the same for us (Hebrews 5:8). The power to overcome in His way through what we suffer comes from the Holy Spirit. Paul says Godly suffering produces perseverance and perseverance character and character hope (Romans 5:3). With strength of character and with integrity anchored in the hope of always living in God's power to overcome, the fruit of the Holy Spirit is revealed in us. We are enabled to love our neighbours as ourselves and to have love, joy, peace, patience, kindness, goodness, faithfulness, gentleness and self-control (Galatians 5:22–23). We become salt and light in this world in obedience to what God is doing (Matthew 5:13–16). This is a wholesome way of living and God will in due course enable us to be healed of everything that gets in the way of it.

This contrasts strongly with how the personality develops without an everyday relationship with God. Without His power to overcome, our natural reactions are not, in themselves, able to transcend the wounds and temptations of this world. Other spiritual paths may capture our hearts but ultimately fail to lead us to His peace. Our natural reasoning may be well informed and logical but it will ultimately prove inadequate if it lacks God's wisdom (Psalm 94:11). Our own ideas of what is good and bad may seem sensible but without the guidance of the Holy Spirit, and the involvement of other people in whom the Spirit lives, we fail to discover the Truth who can empower us to overcome the death-tendency and set us free. Ultimately distress and illness may lead to hopelessness and bitterness, and the ensuing impulsiveness and loss of self-control may spread torment and wretchedness amongst other people. Furthermore, our spirits, souls and bodies are affected so that they reflect the failure to live according to their maker's instructions and they become susceptible to unnecessary corruption.

Relationship

All spiritual beings, both seen and unseen, are social. In general, their closest association is with their own kind, with whom they may most easily establish understanding. Beings of the same kind may fairly easily empathise with each other and know each other. This way species live together in groups within which each individual has identity. Social grouping enables them to be fruitful and to expand their collective influence. Different kinds of creature have different kinds of characteristics, powers and domains.

Species relate to members of other species less easily and with less empathy than to members of their own kind but all animate beings to whom God has given the breath of life (so that they have souls) may to some extent communicate reciprocally both with each other and also with those spiritual beings whom we do not see in physical bodies. For example, a man and his dog may work as a team and both together may sense danger without seeing any actual sign of it; a wolf and a bear who come close together in the wild may have some sort of reciprocity and understanding; demons may leave a man in the presence of Jesus, enter a herd of swine and make them run over a cliff (Mark 5, etc.) and so on.

Personalities are spiritual entities. When they affect or influence each other there is relationship. Relationship is spiritual. Sentient beings have the capacity to sense presence; I believe it is a sixth sense in us. Spiritual presence is in the air we breathe and is discerned in the heart under the control of the mind. If it seems safe and right to do so we may allow the personality of another being to influence and affect us (see 1 John 3:24 and 4:1). Then we shall begin to know that person. And if we allow anyone into our own body sexually we shall inevitably know them and be influenced; our defences will have yielded access to the spiritual influences of whomsoever we have had sex with (see Numbers 25:1–3).

Living relationship is denoted whenever we address another being as "you" in the reasonable expectation of some reciprocal reaction being evoked. Usually we get to know other people gradually so as not to be taken unawares in any way. But, in contrast, relationship with inanimate things is qualitatively different and can never really be expected to evoke any living response. Therefore we address them as "it."

However, we can in practice be said to have a relationship with those inanimate objects which have relevance and meaning for us because of their use or significance to us. The relevance, use and meaning of inanimate objects arise out of their connection with our living relationships, past and present. For example, although you may become attached to the house where you have made a peaceful home, and although the house may evoke memories and passions which give you the illusion of a relationship with it, the sense of relationship comes from the multitude of personal historical and present connections with it, and the spiritual atmosphere consequently attached to the house, whilst essentially the house itself remains an "it," an object. In itself it does not contribute to the changes which may occur in your spirit, soul and body whilst you live there.

Offence may be taken, quite naturally, if a person should be treated impersonally as an "it." This may happen when a person is treated as a function of their job or when a person is stereotyped through prejudice. It can hurt when you are not known for the person you really are. To objectify someone in order to avoid truly personal meeting can be a brutal way of saying "I cannot face really knowing you."

Sometimes, of course, it can be appropriate to avoid knowing too much about someone else. This is why formal manners have evolved. Although to be formally polite is impersonal it is designed not to be offensive.

Out of the complexities of our personal relationships arise all the vicissitudes of life through which we are challenged and changed in character, and through which we contribute to changes in circumstances. Most significant of all are the relationships with our own kind, with other human beings, especially those relationships which involve us most closely. But the most powerful determinant of how our character develops, and of how we behave, is the god whom we effectively worship. Different gods bear different fruits through their relationships with us.

Of course, our relationships with other souls often present difficulties. When there is conflict with someone else we can either defend ourselves by justifying ourselves and criticizing others or we can muster the personal security and humility to look inside ourselves to try to be more truthful about ourselves and about what is going on. We can make enemies by fighting; we can agree to differ; we can pretend to agree but bear secret grudges; or we can keep the conversation going in order to try to work things out. We can try to manage in our own strength, which will inevitably involve gods of the fallen world, or we can call on the one true God for help and lay the situation before Him in the name of Jesus and attend to His guidance (1 Peter 5:7). He is our rock (Psalm 18). He is the way to change and grow in maturity and He is the God of peace. Then circumstances change in their turn, according to God's healing plan.

When our security seems threatened, in order to try to maintain control it is our nature to defend ourselves or to attack. Only if it seems safe to allow another person's influence into our lives do we lower our defences. We have to lower our defences to let God in but it is necessary to be very careful about which god we let in.

How we change

Some people say we change through adopting new ideas and thoughts by changing the mind through being taught better systems of thinking. But people change far more lastingly and profoundly through changing their spiritual allegiance and working it out in the details of everyday life. Just as the Hebrews of the Old Testament could never actually manage to obey their law so, too, people may be influenced by good ideas but do not really change unless they have a change of heart, which is spiritual. In Galatians 3:5 Paul asks, "Does God give you His Spirit and work miracles among you because you observe the law or because you believed what you heard?" Faith is what really changes people and it comes from believing someone who is credible and from adopting their spirit in the heart.

As everyone who has ever been in love knows, the mind is subject to the heart and the heart craves personal relationship much more profoundly than it ever craves impersonal good ideas and more than it craves things. In order to be credible, ideas have to be worked out in practice, in relationships. What seems real depends on who is believed. If you find someone who seems satisfactorily credible you tend to be willing to accept their way of seeing and thinking as part of the truth, although you will test it against what has made sense for you in the past and against what other people believe. What is believed depends on who is believed.

You may even, on occasion, attach yourself quite closely to a person whose way of thinking seems to be particularly relevant, in order to learn and grow. This is how children learn from their parents; and as we mature we often use other parent-figures this way. We allow them to teach us and we tend to copy them. When the relationship has run its course disciples or students usually become independent. Jesus' disciples followed Him like this for three or four years and His Spirit influenced them and changed them. But the course of a relationship with God through Jesus is never finished in this world. Although He may at first seem hidden, He is the most credible person. It is through knowing and loving Him in your heart that you change in the direction of real salvation, your mind changes and situations change for good (Romans 8:28).

In general, as we are guided along a spiritual path we gain knowledge through maturing according to the experience that we are able to receive and make sense of along that path. We are all on one spiritual path or another, whether we acknowledge the fact or not, and we are guided by the people we know and love in our hearts. And we are guided most profoundly by whomsoever we effectively worship, that is by our god or gods.

It is not only the God of Israel whose voice may say behind us "this is the way, walk in it" (Isaiah 30:21). The gods of our mentors will influence us. The god we worship will determine which other people we relate with and will interpret our experience and regulate the knowledge that comes to us through them.

Therefore it is of vital importance to know by name and nature who is really being worshipped in any situation. You may be freely and openly introduced to a god by name or you may be seduced into a relationship without realising what is happening. Film and drama, journalism, art, music and books all try to influence you along some spiritual path or other. If you start making sense of the world in a certain way you are following some spiritual path and unless you can name the spirit whom you are making worthy of such honour you could be said not to know what you are doing. It is insufficient just to say you are guided by a higher power for there are many higher powers, although there is only one with supreme authority.

As you follow a spiritual path the god to whom you have given the power to influence your life imparts a singular nuance to every perception. Thus a system of belief, thought and behaviour develops within you which makes you live a certain way, and which influences other people through you and thereby changes circumstances so as to serve the purposes of that god in this world. Different gods bear different fruit (Matthew 7:15–20).

These days there are many people who are unable to find anyone really credible. They trust no one. Very many people have been betrayed so very many times. So many have no experience of faithfulness or unconditional love. They have never found anyone who can withstand all accusation and criticism and still remain loving and faithful. They have no rock. So they readily believe that everything is relative, good only whilst it lasts and feels all right. They always remain willing to explore new options. Nothing has lasting meaning for them.

They easily adopt any system of belief that seems reasonable and socially acceptable until something else seems better. What they really believe in is cynicism. Cynicism is connected with destruction and despair.

When it seems difficult to make sense of what is going on, and when you do not know what to do or to whom to turn, it may seem expedient to compromise with someone who offers plausible answers which seem to promise to satisfy some pressing needs. But plenty of people are aware of how to manipulate you through the threat of withdrawing what you want. And plenty of people know how to seduce, manipulate and indoctrinate you through supplying what you want. This way you can be used to serve the destructive purposes of some spiritual being or other and sooner or later you may wake up to the fact. If you end up wounded it may only serve to aggravate your sense of meaninglessness and ennui, in which you may even take pride. Your wounds may even enhance the hatred and the envy you may come to feel against those who know the security of peaceful, faithful and loving families.

Systems of thought and belief adopted in such ways, and through such experiences, are never true to the heart because the heart only comes open and alive with love. Without love there is no healing and no meaning true to life. The only God who works through unconditional love is the God you find through Jesus.

With insecurity and fear the heart guards itself, closes and becomes deadened and calloused (see Isaiah 6:9–10). Lies, because they deceive, intuitively cause insecurity and fear. The spiritual person who leads the whole world astray is Satan and he has many demons working for him, some stronger than others.

Many spiritual powers operate in this world to destroy love which is innocent. Deception, deprivation, abuse, curses, and domination are to be found everywhere and they can cause terrible wounds, sometimes even without a person realising that they are wounded. The extent of the damage may only become apparent later when, by the grace of God, the senses cease to be hypnotised and numbed by deception and start to be sensitive to truth.

If we have not allowed the one true loving Father God to show us how to overcome the difficulties which may come our way, some of which may be severe, we are vulnerable. It is necessary for each one of us to develop character and immunity by persevering, with our true Father's guidance, through suffering experiences which are challenging, so as to be sure in our relationship with Him and obedient to Him in all we do and all our other relationships. This way He imparts to us shrewdness, discernment, wisdom, self-control and maturity, which come from being close to Him. After all, He is in charge.

Yet the Bible says "where the Spirit of the Lord is there is freedom" (2 Corinthians 3:17). However, this is not the freedom to do whatever we fancy, and not the freedom which comes from propitiating or conciliating anyone; nor is it freedom from having to conform. It is the freedom of being with our loving Father. Because of the victory won on the cross by the Lord Jesus Christ of Nazareth, God's only begotten Son, we may receive the Holy Spirit and allow ourselves to be guided, healed and protected by Him. Then we can be united in him collectively and yet remain whole individuals each with our singular personality, talents and qualities, without any sense of bondage, so that there is diversity in the unity.

Physiology

A man called Tom was once subjected to a physiological experiment which became famous. Due to a serious injury to his oesophagus, part of his stomach had been exposed on the surface of his abdomen in order to enable him to be fed. So the responses of the internal stomach lining, which are normally hidden, could thereby be observed with the naked eye. When

Tom was deliberately made angry, with "mounting hostility and resentment," it was noted that his stomach lining became very red and engorged. Whereas when he was deliberately made frightened his stomach lining clearly became paler and thinner. The experiment may seem to have been cruel but it provided very clear proof that relationships may affect the living, physical body.

Similarly, we may notice our hearts beating faster when we are anxious and worried and we may discover a strong need to use the toilet when we are frightened. In more subtle ways, too, our body language often betrays emotions, which we may try to hide. So it is apparent that our living bodies change according to the feelings and emotions aroused through our relationships.

Our feelings and emotions may sometimes change without our awareness of the real cause of the change. We may begin to perspire, or get pains in the gut, without really knowing why. But if we can avoid being too defensive, so as to allow our minds to know the truth about how and why our bodies are in fact reacting, we may find that our bodies are confirming what we may already be sensing intuitively about events that are happening. We shall discern atmospheres and influences and know more readily what is going on around us. For instance, we shall know whether or not we are being deceived. In this way our bodies do, in fact, keep us in touch with the world, so it behoves us to listen to them.

Some of the changes in our physiology due to our natural emotional responses may cause worrying physical symptoms. It is surprisingly common, for example, for someone to experience quite severe pain in the lower chest, or in the upper or central abdomen, as a result of loss or rejection. It is common for blocked frustration and tears to cause headache. Disgust may cause vomiting. Embarrassment may cause blushing.

If the emotion is not expressed openly in the light, not admitted to and not confessed to God, and if His response is not received, it may cause illness by being suppressed or even denied.

If such an emotional state persists, or even becomes habitual and associated with set ways of thinking, like chronically suppressed unforgiveness, the body may adapt to the chronic stresses and produce physical discomforts which may disorganise the proper functioning of the body and result in chronic illness.

In the same way it can be understood that all our relationships affect our souls and our bodies. We are physiologically touched by the spirit at the heart of other people when their words and actions get through to us and cause a response. In order to make sense and have meaning they often need time to be digested, which is why we get to know other people gradually. Otherwise their true relevance may not be apparent to us. To assimilate true knowledge of our world requires our critical faculties to be engaged like digestive juices. To respond blindly, without reference to the heart and mind, and without appropriate censorship, can be dangerous because it may lead to being manipulated. The spiritual person we worship determines the activity of our censor, that is our god will tell us what to cut ourselves off from. Thus, the way we are touched and the way we respond is influenced by whichever spiritual being may live in us.

Therefore, if we seek healing it makes sense to get all our relationships, past and present, right with God, and to make Him part of our life and take all our feelings and conflicts to Him, to forgive and be forgiven, and so on (see 1 Peter 5:7). This applies both to physical healing and also to psychological and emotional healing. Whether physically or mentally ill, it is appropriate to get into the deepest repentance possible, perhaps with the help of others. The Holy Spirit can always show us how to do this.

Furthermore, since we inherit in our genes the results of our ancestors' relationships we should endeavour to bring our ancestors' lives to God for healing as well (note Exodus 20:5 and Deuteronomy 23:2). How things were with our parents and ancestors obviously affects us now. Memory of what went on with them in the past was laid down in their bodies and transferred to our genes and inherited, not consciously but in our

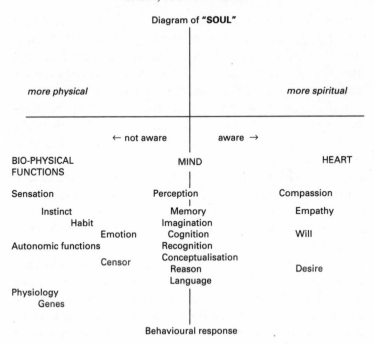

Diagram of **"SOUL"**

| more physical | | more spiritual |

← not aware | aware →

BIO-PHYSICAL FUNCTIONS	MIND	HEART
Sensation	Perception	Compassion
Instinct	Memory	Empathy
Habit	Imagination	
Emotion	Cognition	Will
Autonomic functions	Recognition	
Censor	Conceptualisation	Desire
	Reason	
	Language	
Physiology		
Genes		

Behavioural response

bodies. Because we are usually unaware of most of the details, our prayers about this usually have to be general rather than precise. God has the power to set us free from the sins of our ancestors (see Ezekiel 18).

Relationships are spiritual. The spirit is not separate from the body. (The teaching that body and spirit are two separate realms was the Nicolaitan heresy condemned in the letters to the seven churches in Revelation[1].)

Our spiritual relationships determine our biochemistry, our biophysics and our physiology. Our relationship with the Holy Spirit brings healing. We are people, not machines, and all things are possible to God.

---

[1] I thank the Rev. Dr. Clifford Hill for this information. He referred me to Irenaeus, Adv. Haer. (*Against Heresies*), I:26 and III:10.7.

CHAPTER THREE

HEART

Burden

If I ask you to tell me what is on your heart, you will know what I mean and you will be able to do so if you are willing. If you tell God in Jesus' name about what is on your heart, and ask God to speak relevant healing words into your heart, you will find that peace of heart comes when He does so.

This is more than just expressing heartfelt emotion. You can always find some relief just by getting it off your chest, especially if you do it with someone credible who listens intelligently. Furthermore, you can even see things in a different perspective if you unburden your heart and just listen to yourself. But the response which is truly healing only comes from God.

More than from just dumping your feelings, healing peace comes from hearing and receiving God's reply. A relationship with God, through having accepted Jesus, brings God into your soul. He knows the truth about what is on your heart anyway (Acts 1:24, Hebrews 4:13, etc.) but the process of making yourself accountable to Him causes you to become aware when something in your heart is not right with Him. With love and justice His voice from within your heart will tell you what to do about it. You will know, and what He says will bring peace and healing.

As the relationship with God continues the personal issues of your heart that He reveals may be quite surprising. Sometimes they may even be confusing for a while. As time goes on, things still keep coming up for you to deal with. He forgives and heals if you ask, at the same time specifically acknowledging that Jesus paid the price with His blood for your freedom. He enables you to forgive and to bless and to love those who hurt you. Through the Holy Spirit He gives you His power to resist the devil and effectively to renounce whatever needs to be renounced so that you may be reconciled to Him. This way He changes you and through you other people are influenced. This way the world changes and what is spiritual changes what is physical.

After baptism in Holy Spirit you find you have an ongoing relationship with God wherein nothing that comes into the heart can ultimately be withheld from God's pure Spirit. It is really a struggle and stress to be holding anything back from Him. All the responses of the heart become opened to His Spirit. Moreover, it is impossible to do all the praying in your native tongue. So, as your heart reaches out to communicate with Him, He will enable your tongue to be involved in a private spiritual language that He understands.

If ever I were to have a heart attack (which God forbid!) I hope I would have the nous to open my heart to God, to open every secret place to Him and to seek the help of other people to discover any issue still remaining hidden, about which I may not yet have been open with Him. That this can bring healing and relief to the physical heart may be proved by ministering in this way to people with physical diseases of the heart, including angina and heart failure. You may discover that an anxious heart really does weigh a person down (Proverbs 12:25) and that troubles and anxieties really can cause the heart to fail

(Psalm 40:12) and that the heart really may falter in horror (Isaiah 21:4) and be physically hardened by sin's deceitfulness (Hebrews 3:12–13) and so on.

Unburdening the heart truthfully, forgiving and being forgiven and putting the heart right with God, brings peace and gets rid of what gets in the way of God's healing of the spirit, soul and body. I once knew a man who was so stubborn that he went so far as to have heart transplant surgery instead of putting the affairs of his heart right with God, which in his case would probably have worked better and which is a rather drastic way of having a change of heart.

If we love other people and walk in the light of God's revelation in this world our hearts will inevitably be wounded and we shall suffer (see 1 Peter 4:19). But through walking with God in this open way, in the light, always seeking reconciliation with Him, we can constantly be working free. Through exposing the life of our heart of flesh to God we can discover how our relationships, which are spiritual, correlate with the functions of the physical heart. Confession and repentance when you are sick, with the help of other people if necessary (James 5:16) can often make the connection clear.

A grave insult, with a damning opinion of a person's abilities, is liable to do physical damage if it is all taken to heart. If someone says "she took it to heart" the fact is that her heart may be affected, and often not only her heart. What is taken to heart is embodied. The heart knows if something is received like this. If it seems impossible to forgive the insult, and if the lies are not corrected by replacing them with God's opinion, the curse may wound the heart and the body and cause pain or even death. However, if she opens her heart to God and tells Him her pain, He will comfort her. He will reveal that she must accept that His Son Jesus became a curse for her (Galatians 3:13). So she should break the curse in Jesus' name then forgive and bless those who have cursed her and accept God's healing for her body, with thanks. Then she is free and her heart is free. She has overcome the natural reaction of her heart, which would probably have caused much bitterness and sin, and maybe serious physical illness. She has overcome the attack of the devil on her life.

Similar reasoning applies to other parts of the body. If you say "I cannot stomach that" but you believe that you have to do so in the circumstances, it would be reasonable to suppose that you could consequently develop some trouble with your stomach, unless you put the whole situation right with God. If you have sexual anxieties and fantasies it is reasonable to suppose that your reproductive system (prostate gland or womb, etc.) could be physically affected. If you cannot bear dirt and do not know what to do with it your bowel (colon) could be affected, and so on. The fact that we refer to distinct parts of our physical body in our everyday thought, language and behaviour indicates their functional involvement in our everyday relationships. There is a real connection between the physical organ and the spiritual relationships which involve it. Just as the smell of a good dinner affects the digestive system so too matters pertaining to inspiration may affect the lungs and the affairs of the heart affect the heart and the part of the body most significantly engaged will always be the most affected. This may naturally be the part of the body where there is most conflict. If the heart is troubled it will probably be the most affected.

When we constantly walk and talk with God, and confess our human responses to whatever affects us (like, "She is making me feel sick, Lord!" "Help!" "I forgive her!" "Please heal me!" and so on) healing comes as we resist the devil in Jesus' name and submit to how it is with God and put ourselves right with Him (James 4:7). Our human responses include the physical responses of the parts of our body as well as our thoughts and emotions. God will heal wounds and illnesses after the response of the flesh is confessed, the natural reaction renounced and the power of the devil broken. If your eyes are offensive to God, put the flesh to death and let Him heal them (Matthew 5:29–30)!

The responses and activities of all parts of the physical body are relayed through the heart, and then through the mouth (Matthew 12:34–35). Consequently it is the heart that always has to be unburdened.

More than a pump

In the Holy Bible there are many cogent references to the significance of parts of the body. Symbolic use is made of how they may be affected by what goes on. In Exodus 28:30 Aaron the chief priest wears representations of the twelve tribes of Israel over his heart when he comes into God's presence, signifying his spiritual burden. In Philippians 1:7 Paul says he holds the church at Philippi in his heart. In Revelation 10:9–11 God's words turn the prophet's stomach sour. In Isaiah 48:4 the prophet describes Israel's stubbornness in terms of the sinews in their neck being made of iron. In Psalm 147:10 the legs of a man signify strength and agility. There are those footnotes in English Bibles which say, "The meaning of the Hebrew for this clause is uncertain," although we can guess that what is meant is opening the bowels. In 2 Samuel 5:8 David tells his men to defeat the enemy through overcoming their watershaft, which was not only metaphorical! In Matthew 5:29 Jesus is recorded as saying that offence could be caused through the eye.

The Hebrew language is down to earth and used for vivid effect. Meaning becomes cogent through speaking openly of the involvement of the parts of the human body with everyday relevance. There is a notable absence of the detached scepticism, common in technologically sophisticated cultures, whereby facts which make sense in the heart are considered less reliable and less useful than knowledge which is classified, measured and reflected upon objectively in the mind. Consequently in Hebrew thought human experience is full of immediate relevance which relates directly to the human body. "Now my heart is troubled . . ." (John 12:27) conveys a powerful experience with which we can immediately empathise. The Hebrew mind in Biblical times seems to have been more connected with the physical body than is common in modern technological cultures and they seem to have been more sure of the meaning of their experience and therefore less inclined to dismiss some experiences as beyond the pale, mad, or in need of objective analysis.

Thus the heart is more than the muscular pump for blood abstractly described by modern medical science. It is the heart of the soul. It is sensitive to the spirit of every relationship and responds with feelings and may be filled with passion, it may be prompted and moved, it may gently yield or be hardened, it may be divided or steadfast, it is the repository of thoughts, attitudes and knowledge, it is the seat of desire and purpose, it may be wise and discerning and may instruct us in our dreams, it may be given, lost and won.

We still refer to the heart in these ways in our own everyday language, just as people did when the Bible as written. But nowadays we forget to connect colloquial references to the heart with our actual physical hearts because we have forgotten how to unburden our hearts to God. We have fallen into doubt and unbelief and have put too much faith in abstract scientific technology to be able to trust what we say.

All these qualities of the heart derive from the spiritual sensitivity of the heart and its central place in gathering the responses of the living body. The heart collects the responses of the soul and it is from the heart that we speak (Matthew 12:34b) and from the heart that we are essentially motivated (Proverbs 27:19).

Hardness and division

The heart responds to whatever involves the person and the heart is involved in every aspect of our every relationship. If you do something with your body without being fully and freely committed to what you are doing (that is, if your heart is not freely in it) your heart will be divided because it is not ultimately possible to separate heart and living body. Denial, however, can give you the illusion that the heart is cut out from the proceedings and need not be in it, although in truth the denial is protecting the heart from reality by making it insensitive and numb. Denial is a powerful spirit. When the heart is numb the person does not have to feel the effects of what is going on. The numbness of denial shields the human spirit, soul and body from distress, conflict and trauma. People sometimes take drugs (legal or illegal) to assist the anaesthesia. When the Bible speaks of a divided heart this is the origin of it. Being divided between being in what is going on and being out of it puts a strain on the heart which wounds the heart. The numbness will prevent any awareness of the wound until it is safe enough to let go of the numbness and become aware of what is underneath. The heart's natural response to what was occurring remains concealed until an appropriate time and place is found for its release.

Conflict and trauma come from what is going on being too much to allow or make sense of. It may be too much for various reasons. It may be that nothing like this has ever happened before. Alternatively it may be that things like this have indeed happened before and have not been adequately healed, so that unhealed wounds, defences and prejudices prevent wholeheartedness and salt is rubbed into the wounds, as it were. It may be that the pain and devastation of what is going on are far too great to be coped with all at once. It may even be that one's very life depends on not being too aware. Or it may be that the desires and lusts of the flesh override the sensibilities of the heart. In all these situations the heart may go numb. Denial and numbness can be a natural protective response of the heart but, as with all emotional responses, a demon spirit will take advantage, if able to do so, in order to make the denial and the desire habitual and permanently damaging.

Thus, the heart may go numb from external assaults from circumstances outside the person, such as when a person is shocked or forcefully assaulted, abused or dominated. And it may also go numb from internal assaults from within the person's heart and mind, from strong desires and lustfulness or from a prejudiced and over-defensive mind. Overriding lust and dominating desire and prejudice are usually driven by demonic spirits which have been able to form a parasitic alliance with the person and which thus effectively become part of the person. Demonised people may believe themselves to be wholehearted in what they do but in the light of God they will be seen to be driven, not free. People may joke about their demons but if they are honest they will realise that they cause real trouble and they would be better off without them. Jesus enables people who come to Him to be rid of their demons.

Take an extreme example, such as rape. The victim's heart is numbed in self-protection. The perpetrator's heart is numbed with the lust of sexual violence. The demons will usually have got in through violence done to the perpetrator sometime in the past. Much later, the hearts of both may, by God's grace, come to yield to His healing love. To turn to Him for healing in the name of Jesus is to repent. It is painful. As their hearts yield, out will pour terrible pain and agonising confessions. To confess is to admit the Spirit of truth into your body and to speak out from the heart the burden your body is carrying so that God's healing and forgiveness may come in. Healing is possible in the name of Jesus because Jesus bore our pain and iniquity on the cross and overcame it by rising from the dead the third day. Both victim and perpetrator may find God's healing by opening their hearts to Him and making their confession from the bottom of the heart, by accepting Jesus as their Lord and then commanding the demons out in Jesus' name, and allowing God's healing into their very flesh.

A heart which cannot be wholly open because it is divided and callous is a heart which cannot be wholly given in relationship because of secrets. The secrets contain the responses of the heart which are concealed because they were too much, too painful, too dreadful, too shameful, too terrifying, too intoler-able, too confusing, too embarrassing, to bring to light at the time they first occurred. Because of them, the person is not entirely free to know and to be known or to love and to be loved. And those secrets will always exert a hidden influence until that person allows the Holy Spirit in and God's light is shed upon them, enabling them to be unlocked and to be put right with God (1 John 1:7). Thus Jesus breaks the power of repeated sin.

The hearts of some people have been so frequently assaulted, both from without and from within, that they become callous and all contact with the heart's sensitivity is lost. So the real person is hidden. But God knows what is in the heart of each one of us (Acts 1:24). He can penetrate the mask and He can make the deepest contact within the heart of anyone who asks.

Callous people hurt other people. Psalm 73:21–22 tells how a grieved heart and embittered spirit may make a person sense-less, ignorant and brutal. Sometimes it is only when hurtful people are met by other people who show the forgiveness and kindness which come from Jesus that their hearts are touched enough for them to begin to realise the extent to which they have hurt others. Such kindness must be shrewd in order to avoid being manipulated and it is safest if it is shown openly, within a group or community, so that people may be openly accountable to each other (Matthew 5:16). Jesus makes it pos-sible to hate the sin but love the sinner. Where there is a spirit of kindness, forgiveness and truth, hardened people can some-times begin to reveal the painful and confused secrets of their own hearts, and make sense of them, and accept Jesus. Then they can bring their calloused hearts, which have caused so much pain to themselves and to others, to God for healing of the real root of their trouble. Healing the heart like this trans-forms people much more profoundly than simply retraining the mind through psychological techniques or through dogma.

Therefore Jesus should be given much more help to be better

known, and a much more honourable and dignified place than is usual, in hospitals and prisons.

Allegiance and influence

A calloused heart becomes hardened physically and, because it is essentially a divided heart, it may one day break, either with emotion or physically. Either heartbrokenness or heart attack become more possible if the heart is being pulled two or more ways by being deeply attached to two or more people who make conflicting demands. This may indeed be the cause of either a nervous breakdown or of a coronary thrombosis. Physical illness is more likely if there is persistent defensiveness, fear and denial.

Personal relationships, and the heart's consequent attachments, affect the heart physically. So how we live and whom we relate to become reflected in how our bodies function. And when our lives are wrong with God there is physical dysfunction. When God is allowed to heal the dysfunction the good function of the body may sometimes return.

It is natural for the human heart to seek to open to other people truthfully and lovingly and to respond to other beings at least in such a way as to seek some understanding with them, if not to join with them. However, the heart can only be open and free like this when there is truth with healing love, without any conditions or constraints. If there seems to be no-one with whom to relate easily the heart tends to close up, and it may eventually die. The nature of the commitment of the heart (that is, how easily it may be given and may receive) affects the physical heart. If there is too much hate it hardens and if there is too much fear it perishes. Fear and hate are natural responses to threats; but demons may use such natural responses to make them habitual and then they will try to prevent a person getting free of the habit of fearing or hating, or whatever. When there is a pervasive atmosphere of fear or hate it is always demonic but disciples of Jesus may use the authority He gives them to overcome those demons and be rid of them in Jesus' name.

Truth and love, in contrast, come from God. He has made our hearts in such a way that in love they come alive with joy, like His heart does. More than anything else, more than objects, more than any addiction, the human heart craves truthful and loving relationships in which to find the freedom to love and be loved and to know and be truly known. Love brings ease to the heart but only when the love has no deceitful conditions attached and is right with God.

The human heart naturally becomes attached to whomsoever is familiar or loved; but freedom is only found through attachment to our creator – Father God. The heart may also naturally become attached to whatever objects of desire are associated with any relationship. But God says we should have no idols and worship Him only, and Jesus tells us to leave everything to follow Him (Exodus 20:4, Matthew 19:16–30, etc.). Nevertheless, any threat of the loss of any important attachment may cause the heart naturally to respond with fear. And if times have been hard and there has generally never been much love, any attachment to what seems good, and the fear of losing it, may be all the more severe and desperate. A heart which has been chronically deprived of love and truth will tend to cling strongly to whatever makes it feel good or seems to bring some ease. Only gradually, as we grow in maturity, do we become able to know what is enough for us, and able to release (if necessary) people and things we have become attached to, and so develop substantial faith. We shall never be perfect, however, until we live in the new Jerusalem (Revelation 21 and 22).

A baby naturally clings to the breast from which warm nourishing milk comes with love, but in due course the child is weaned and takes some solid food and discovers that the breast is not the only source of goodness. After solid food comes spiritual food. Provided there is enough love, and enough parental recognition of the developing needs and personality, the child takes what is necessary and is then able to relinquish successive attachments and move on to maturity. One day, a young adult becomes independent and sets up in a separate home.

But if there has been chronic deprivation of love, of truth, of recognition, or of meeting appropriate physical needs, the heart will naturally continue to crave what has been lacking until some satisfaction can be found. Then, when some approximation to what is needed is found, there may be an excessive emotional investment in it for fear of losing it. I once knew a man who had accepted the sexual love of other men, which had become addictive, because he had never been able to find healing for his profound sense that his love was rejected by his mother because she deserted him as a tiny baby. This way the heart becomes bound in attachments which the devil can easily use to manipulate, dominate and control, so as to proceed to wound both self and others.

Furthermore, when the attachment to someone deeply loved is prematurely broken, the pain and confusion may sometimes stop the heart from ever being given to anyone else again. Thank God that the first disciples did not react in this way to Jesus' death because they had seen Him resurrected! For some people, however, it may seem impossible to believe it is better to have loved and lost than never to have loved at all. So the heart becomes numb and stops loving.

God can heal these situations by supplying the real needs of anyone who will turn to Jesus in repentance and faith. But He depends on the hospitality of His people. There are very many wounded people who need other people to be like the good Samaritan and like the innkeeper on the Jericho road (Romans 12:13).

Sometimes it is necessary to allow a person to love you for a while, and to be attached for a while without expecting the relationship to be equally mature, and to meet that person always in truth and good faith and with God's wisdom, until it is possible for that person to move on. Such apprenticeship or discipleship or therapeutic relationships are eventually relinquished quite naturally provided there be no sin and no wounding, and provided the Spirit of God remains the guide. The first disciples had this sort of relationship with Jesus.

Jesus kept His closest disciples with Him for at least three years and he was very patient with them. He was not lonely because He was so intimate with His Father. And He did not just fill their heads full of knowledge. Rather, they found healing and changed personally in body, soul and spirit through knowing and loving Him. Through remaining in relationship with Him they grew in wisdom and maturity. Then, when they were baptised in Holy Spirit they were ready to be fully open to His person living in them (Ephesians 1:13–14). We, too, can help other people to heal and grow and prepare to receive Jesus fully if we are prepared to disciple in His name those the Lord sends to us.

God loves us in this way. We are only little children with Him but His love is always faithful, eternal and unconditional. Provided we each remain in this sort of loving attachment to Him in this world we eventually get free after we have passed through death and when we join Him in His eternal kingdom.

Guarding the heart

When we allow His Spirit to guide us, God shows us how to negotiate the nature of our relationships and attachments so that each one of us may change to become more like Him by loving Him with all our hearts and loving our neighbours as ourselves. He knows we need the company and help of other people and He allows us to marry (Genesis 2:20–24) and to live in families (Psalm 68:6) and communities (Numbers 1:2) and nations (Genesis 10:1 – 11:9).

He wants to redeem us so that we become His devoted people, loving Him, knowing Him, close to Him, faithful to Him, as He is to us, and faithful to one another. His heart has gone out to us and He wants to win our hearts. To this end He has made covenants with us (Genesis 6:18) to guarantee that His purpose is being worked out amongst us. "If we are faithless He will remain faithful" (1 Timothy 2:13).

When our hearts have been given to Him they are free. But we are easily deceived (Jeremiah 17:9–10) and when our hearts are given wrongly to other gods, to other people, and to things, we may readily involve them in attachments and entrapments which are damaging both to ourselves and to others.

God tells people not to unite with anyone else in any sort of covenant, or with any sort of oath, because we shall always be held to the terms of any covenants or oaths by the divine power under whose auspices they are made. To make a covenant implies coming together in binding agreement in the name of a god who will always make sure the agreement is kept. The sacrifice of a life, which may be symbolised by blood, is always demanded for a real covenant to be in effect because gods demand lives (see Hebrews 9:16–28). If you break a covenant it can cost you your life, and it will certainly affect your heart.

However, in view of the inevitable bondage between hearts and souls which comes from coming together as one flesh in physical sexual intercourse[1], God allows human beings to make one particular covenant one with another, namely the covenant between a man and a woman in marriage (Malachi 2:14). This is so that our marriages on earth may become like the marriage of the Lord Jesus with His people, and our families like God's family. In Christian marriage each life has been laid down, both by having been given to God and by being given to each other, and each spouse covenants with the other to be faithful to their physical unity.

God's nature is to be loving, merciful and faithful but He is also jealous and just. He will withdraw His blessing and

---

[1] If your heart is not in it what are you doing?

protection if we renege on a commitment we have made to Him. Where He is ignored and where there is serious sin He may act in judgement so as to tell people clearly that He is to be reckoned with, and to tell us that He is concerned for us and loves us with all His heart and wants to draw us to Himself, and to tell us that He wants us to have a loving, personal relationship with Himself so that His presence may be known amongst us.

When we truly love Him we shall have the desire to be faithful to Him and to make Him the only God we worship. Furthermore when we have received baptism in Holy Spirit our bodies are temples of the Holy Spirit (1 Corinthians 6:19) and the Holy Spirit living in us will always be telling us that our bodies are not to be defiled. Consequently we shall not easily give our hearts to making any agreements or allegiances with other people, or with other spiritual beings, which would dishonour our one true God in any way. We shall not unite ourselves carelessly with anyone else, nor shall we enter into the spirit of any event without discerning the spiritual influences which could thereby come into our hearts. The Holy Spirit will guide us into taking care to protect ourselves.

Covenants which have been wrongly made can, in fact, be broken, albeit often with difficulty, through unconditionally accepting the authority of the New Covenant in the blood of Jesus which has power over all other covenants, oaths, agreements and allegiances. Provided a person turns to Jesus in total repentance and commitment, and provided that all bondages, all attachments which are wrong with Him, have been definitively and permanently relinquished, that person may be set free.

Jesus says "Simply let your 'Yes' be 'Yes' and your 'No', 'No'; anything beyond this comes from the evil one" (Deuteronomy 23:21–23, Matthew 5:33–37). Nevertheless He expects any agreement or commitment to be made truthfully and wholeheartedly. When all our relationships are right with Him in this way they bring peace into our personal hearts, into our lives and into our communities.

The best and most concentrated piece of detailed guidance about guarding the heart is in Proverbs. The first few chapters tell us to fear and to trust the Lord and to allow Him to direct our paths – which means really knowing Him in our hearts. They tell us that in order to remain in this relationship our hearts must yield to Him tenderly, like children with their loving father (Proverbs 4:3, Luke 18:17). They say that through our relationship with God we shall receive His wisdom so that we put away corrupt talk, perversity and wickedness and hold on to Him in the face of all temptation. We shall avoid sexual sin, and avoid making pledges, and be discrete, and do our work diligently. We shall avoid deception, pride and bloodshed, and hate evil, and shall be able to fix our eyes on what is right. "Above all else," says Solomon, "guard your heart, for it is the wellspring of life." (4:23.) "In the paths of those who are perverse are thorns and snares but if you guard your soul you keep well away from them." (22:5.)

In the hearts of very many people there is tremendous personal deprivation and grief, and many other wounds, bondages and secrets which are mostly hidden and unmet (Luke 8:17). Multitudes need to come to their senses, unburden their hearts and find healing. They should be able to find the Lord Jesus Christ of Nazareth, the great physician and heart specialist, amongst His true disciples. Otherwise they can call on Him by name and He will come and meet with them (Revelation 3:20). The prayers at the end of this book will help them. Let them receive Him as Lord in their hearts. Then the Holy Spirit, the comforter, will lead them, when their hearts are tender, closer and closer to God who loves them. He will show them how to guard their hearts in future. Then their hearts will find peace and joy and they will find themselves spontaneously offering thanks and praise.

CHAPTER FOUR

MIND

Structure

Since it is not seriously conceivable that inert matter could ever think, and since the mind is composed of thoughts, the mind cannot be a function solely of the material body. Nor, for the same reason, can it be a function merely of the biochemistry and anatomy of the brain. Nevertheless, we know that what comes to mind affects our material bodies. Thoughts are associated both with our feelings and with our physical activity. Thoughts are not purely ethereal and spiritual; they connect with the real person living in a body and relating with other people and things in this world. Therefore the mind is a function of the living principle, that is of the soul (see 1 Corinthians 2:10–11, also Mark 7:21–23).

A person's mind consists of all that may be held in the mind of the individual. What comes to mind at any particular moment is usually connected with what is currently going on for the person, that is with the matter which is currently in hand. The mind becomes focused with vigilance on the processes that are relevant for the accomplishment of the current desire and will of the heart in relation to what is in hand.

The mind guards itself against threats and distractions by censoring unwanted material. In order to avoid confusion and anxiety the mind maintains a state of vigilance by which any thoughts which seem irrelevant or dangerous are censored in order to cut them out of awareness.

There are occasions, however, when thoughts (or sometimes voices) which have no apparent connection with matters in hand persist in intruding into consciousness. In order to discover where they come from it is necessary, first of all, not to dismiss them. Then it is possible to ask God – in the name of the Lord Jesus Christ of Nazareth, His Son, the saviour of mankind – to help to make sense of them. Such thoughts can always be found to come from significantly unfinished, unhealed business and to be associated with unhealed emotion. The unfinished business may be in oneself or in someone else (physical or purely spiritual) to whom one is spiritually attached. Spirit speaks into the mind from the heart, sometimes even with a voice which is only perceived within. Thoughts which intrude into consciousness may, or may not, in some way be discovered to be related to the matter upon which the mind has been focusing. And God, who is Spirit, always has unfinished business with us in this world.

Here's a simple example: I am writing this several hours after having been poignantly reminded of my father, who died some years ago, and thoughts about my father intrude into my consciousness now and then as I concentrate on this writing. Although the origin of such intrusive thoughts may not always be so obvious, they come from past business which is emotional, about which we do not have total peace and which is not fully reconciled to God. Perhaps I have to grieve for my father some more and take more to God for healing. When God heals He gives peace and when I shall have come fully into the peace of God concerning my father I shall have received most of the wisdom which God wants to give me through having known my father.

If I were working in a more public place, where slavish vigilance toward the task in hand was absolutely demanded, I may feel it necessary to put thoughts about my father totally out of my mind. In fact I would probably do this automatically in such a situation. Then nobody would know there was anything under the surface of my mind and I would wear a dutiful face for work. My thoughts about my father would be suppressed so that I could get on with my work and I may well forget about him until something reminded me again. An individual is by no means always aware of all that is in the mind nor, in general, are friends and acquaintances.

Nevertheless, it is probable that my wife, because she knows me intimately, would notice that there was something on my mind which I was letting neither myself nor others know about. Intimacy over an extended period of time, with the spiritual gift of discernment, is necessary for people collectively to have a fair idea of what is really going on, including the undercurrents. This is why it makes more sense for people not to be isolated but rather to live in community.

If many troublesome issues should be put out of mind through calculated determination (will-power) when they have not been completely made right with God, the mind will not be at peace. The reason for inner distress may, however, not be obvious. The face the person presents to the world may seem plausibly calm and collected and the person may be unaware of any inner tension, although it is often subtly revealed to others in body language. We can usually deny our troubles and act a part with a stiff upper lip if it should seem appropriate to do so.

Only a minute fraction of all that is available to the individual mind can ever be conscious or apparent at any given moment because censorship and will-power push most of the material out of mind. At any one time most of a person's mind is hidden. Some of the hidden mind comes into consciousness in association with whatever matter is currently in hand. And some of the hidden mind comes near the surface of awareness when, despite the business which is mainly holding the attention, there is some currently pressing emotional engagement with it. This has been called "the subconscious". Otherwise, the rest of the hidden mind is "unconscious" and relevant issues from it are called into awareness only when they become recognised in connection with some matter in hand to which attention comes to be given.

In order for underlying, hidden truths from a person's mind to come out into the light, with whatever lack of peace may be associated with them, it is necessary to make hospitable, intimate time and space with other people who are trusted to be attentive without imposing their own troubles or misconstruing or abusing the relationship, where constraints and fears and defences may be laid aside, where the heart may be unburdened freely and emotions may be accepted. Sufficient time and space like this, for the opening up, containment and healing of trouble, are necessary for sanity. Often you only get a clear grasp of what to bring to God for healing when you have talked it through with other people. However, as you get older you may find that the wisdom of others has been built into your own mind sufficiently for there to be less need to talk.

There is an important contrast between the world of personal experience, private thoughts and intimate relationships on the one hand and the the more impersonal world of functional efficiency, getting jobs done and creating social order on the other (Matthew 10:38–42). Underlying thoughts may more easily come into awareness ("come to mind") when you are informally at ease. However, when it is important for business to be attended to, exigency and calculation push selected thoughts which seem reasonable in the circumstances into the forefront of the mind. Then reasonable thoughts and logical deductions may exert controls on the hidden parts of the mind and suppress them. Whilst the unconscious and subconscious are suppressed by exigency, access to the unfinished business of the hidden parts of the mind is denied, so healing is not possible.

So in order to know and be in touch with the real person behind the face it is necessary to have some intimacy and ease. And this is only possible if it is safe and no-one is going to take serious advantage should your self-protective defences be relaxed. Formal and polite relationships may suffice for routine business but each one of us needs a time and a place in our day for releasing our defences and for rather uncomfortable, imprecise, messy, intimacy with those amongst whom we dwell. We each need time and space for the opening out of issues which have been hidden. And what is hidden comes into the light not only through discussion but also through arts and pastimes and skills. To bring what has been in the dark into the light we need space where the relevance of our expression may be accepted by other people who are faithful and truthful, who care about us without abusing us, and who can allow us gently to find our way to reconciliation with God.

Households and families, where people live together intimately, were never intended by God to be full only of pleasure and entertainment, nor to be formal, but rather to be messy places of nourishment, care and wisdom under the headship of a father whose own head would be the Lord Jesus Christ (Job 21:21, 1 Timothy 5:8, 1 Corinthians 11:3, etc.). It is to be accepted that Christians may sometimes need to grieve, mourn and wail and travail in repentance (Romans 8, James 4:7–10, 1 Peter 4:17) and that it may take time to make sense of what is going on (Philippians 3:12).

Sometimes it may even be necessary for some people to leave their own homes for the sake of following Jesus (Luke 18:29). Sometimes they may have been driven out of their homes and out of their minds with apparently unfinishable business. Therefore, for those who are seeking the peace of mind which only comes through the Lord Jesus Christ (John 14:27, 2 Timothy 1:7) it is necessary within the church for there to be households which are hospitable to other Christians in such a way as to enable people to be free enough to get into whatever they need to get out of, and to work through it all in order to bring it into the light and bring it to God for healing. Healing the mind involves truthful intimacy with other people before God.

Whatever has been personally experienced will have left an imprint in the mind according to its perceived significance. The interpretation of whatever is sensed is made through connecting with this memory imprint and with the understanding of past experience through which it may be recognised. Consideration of it is guided by currently influential relationships both with human and also with purely spiritual beings. New insight, inspiration, imagination and consequent creativity, thus spring both from past experience and also from past and present living relationships, which are spiritual (all relationship is spiritual). The mind is made up, and understanding develops, as concepts are formed and used.

The individual mind essentially receives thoughts from past experience and from the influence of a person's currently significant relationships. Thus what can be received and known by the mind will be limited both by incompleteness and imperfection of the sense already made of past experience and also by the relationships we make, both human and spiritual. However, our understanding may change through opening out various aspects in intimate relationship with other human and spiritual beings, and allowing something of their influence to change our perception. We may do this person to person or through reading what another person has written, or by allowing their spiritual influence to prevaiil in our hearts, and so on. God's understanding has no limit (Psalm 147:5) and He may impart His understanding to us through other people, if we are able to allow it and receive it, as His Spirit living in us alerts us to what He is saying through them.

Past experience which has not been fully reconciled to God, and about which God's peace has not been fully received, will distort the activity of a person's mind and will consequently distort behaviour. Spiritual influences, too, which do not accord with the nature of the one true God who made us in His image, will also distort the mind and behaviour. Such distortions will cause dysfunction and tend to generate sickness.

Wisdom

Our minds become intelligent by enquiring, with God's grace, into the truthful origins of issues which come into our lives and of thoughts which interest or distract us, or which intrude, or which cause us anxiety or discomfort. If our world never changes, or if we should become so discouraged as to lose all hope in the face of challenges, we do not become wise. In order to gain wisdom and maturity we generally use our troubles (Romans 5:3–4). It is wise, too, to digest and know the godly wisdom of our fathers because it saves us from having to learn again what they already learned. Reinventing the wheel, as it were, is not only a waste of time but may also be exceedingly foolish and dangerous. Learning the hard way is by no means usually necessary.

Matters which disturb us cause us to try somehow or other to gain peace about them. Although the relevance of disturbing thoughts may not be clear, it is often difficult to ignore them despite the discomfort of further enquiry. Peace and understanding eventually come through bringing the relevant issues out into the light and asking God about them and waiting for His answer (Matthew 7:13). This may be a tortuous process, but if we find no time for such reflection and concentrate narrowly, in preference, on our social obligations, and on everyday matters which we already understand, our minds may soon become so full of unfinished business that we avoid reflection altogether because it seems too confusing, disturbing and threatening. Then if sometime or other we happen to fall into some sort of reverie, we may find to our consternation that there seems to be too much unfinished business in the mind for us to make sense of. This may lead us to try to avoid being alone with nothing to do in case uncomfortable thoughts come into the mind. Restlessness and superficiality will betray our weakness and lack of faith. We may even develop a fear of going outside or a fear of going mad.

Furthermore, all unhealed material which is not allowed into conscious awareness, and which is therefore subconscious or unconscious and in the dark, will persistently be influencing our thoughts without our being aware of the fact. Issues from the hidden part of the mind automatically influence the way we experience and understand events as they occur in the present; they automatically colour our perception, cognition and behaviour.

Lasting peace is only found when the unfinished business of the mind is brought out into the open and truthfully told to God and when His forgiveness and His sense and His healing are accepted. It behoves the Christian to be continually engaged in this process of repentance and healing the mind (which is "renewing" the mind, as in Romans 12:2) in order to maintain sanity and in order to make wise decisions. After what is hidden in the mind has been brought out into the light and made right with God, it will be found to have been the cause of distortions, distractions, mistakes, and forgetfulness in speech, decision-making and behaviour. But God forgives and heals and saves. As Paul says, when your body is offered to God as a living sacrifice, and truth is lived out with humility in obedience, you may be transformed by the renewing of your mind (Romans 12:1–2).

If we fall into the trap of dealing with any thoughts and feelings by popular rules such as "that is best forgotten" or "what the eye does not see the heart does not grieve over", our minds and bodies may be expected to bear the consequences of our mistake. Not only may we inadvertently become unadventurous and prejudiced through such simplistic controls which we shall have imposed upon our own minds in order to avoid facing certain uncomfortable issues, but also our minds may eventually become quite tormented with all the business which we have, in truth, felt unable to consider. Furthermore, the physical effects of too much unfinished business may become manifested in chronic physical disease.

In some cultures similar socially imposed controls are represented by totems, that is, by demons, signified by idols of one sort or another, who demand appeasement if their controls should be infringed. In a truly Christian culture, however, "There is nothing concealed that will not be disclosed, or hidden that will not be made known" (Luke 12:2). Christian wisdom and maturity develop through continuing to apply the guidance of the Holy Spirit to material which is uncomfortable, even to material which is generally taboo (Ephesians 5:8–14). In this, He is our comforter. He makes it possible for us to suffer because He gives us real hope. So we find healing and make righteous decisions.

This way, by the grace of God, a person is enabled both to tolerate more anxiety and also to have more understanding. The Lord makes a person more imaginative, more creative and more flexible to obey the promptings of the Spirit. With godly wisdom the mind becomes more open, and less closed, and the heart becomes more generous and more discerning (see Proverbs 1 to 9). Although this does not make a person conform to the pattern of this world, it may make them shrewd.

As the mind is made clear through the application of the blood of Jesus to matters that arise, the mind may be renewed by Holy Spirit, who is the only wise God (Romans 16:27). Then a person may receive divine wisdom and develop intelligent discernment to learn and to apply knowledge in a manner no longer limited by natural talent, experience or education.

Different spiritual paths, however, produce their own different sorts of maturity and their own different fruit (Matthew 7:16, 20). The significant factor is who you look to for revelation (Matthew 6:22–23). Because it is so easy for us to be deceived, the deity chosen to become involved in lightening your path should be unequivocally named. Lucifer accuses and deceives and works through fear but Jesus, the light of the world, saves and works through love (John 10:10).

Memory

A person automatically connects the business of what is going on in the present with similar personal experience of the past. Prior experiences have a determining effect on future behaviour and first experiences are formative. How you do something now depends on how you learned to do something similar in the past. In similar situations, whenever a pattern of events is recognised, present behaviour becomes similar to that of the past.

However, if the mind is sufficiently flexible, a new interpretation may be put on what was learned in the past, according to what seems appropriate for the present. Thus current thoughts, and the person's consequent behaviour, often arise from the living spiritual re-interpretation of the past in the light of the present.

For example, I remember from when I was a child that my prayerful mother once had a very distressed lady-friend from our church to come to live with us for a while, with the blessing of the local doctor who also attended the church. I remember this lady spending a lot of time in her bedroom, often talking with my mother, often tormented, often weeping, and I remember her trying to kill herself once or twice, which distressed my mother enormously so that she pleaded with the lady and eventually this stopped. After some weeks that lady came through the worst of what she had to go through and returned to her grateful husband in a more peaceful state. I met her husband again recently, after many years, and he expressed genuine gratitude for the healing my mother had ministered to his wife, all those years ago, by the grace of God.

Because of what I learned from my mother then I have often, in later life, quite easily found faith for the healing of severe disturbances of mind and have become quite convinced that this healing work is the business of the church. My own past childhood experience has been reinterpreted through the guidance of the Holy Spirit in the light of the present needs of people who have come my way.

Some sort of record of what has been experienced in the past seems to be laid down in the body, particularly in the brain, but also probably somehow involving the structure of ribonucleic acid in the cells of every tissue. The record connects with memory of how past experience was understood and responded to.

When a similar pattern of events occurs in the present, this physical aspect of memory becomes reactivated, and is subconsciously recognised, but it usually becomes reinterpreted by the spirit of the person in the light of present circumstances. The memories, thoughts and responses associated with the past experience may then be suitably modified. In fact the whole understanding of what happened in the past may sometimes change as a consequence of the reinterpretation of similar events in the present. Then the memory changes, including the physical record.

There are times, however, when a past memory may be so significant, vivid and unhealed that, when something happens which subconsciously reminds the person of it, the old responses are re-enacted automatically. Then a person may find themselves playing out an old scenario over which they seem to have no self-control. In the case of the experience of severe physical or emotional trauma, the old shock may need God's healing before there can be any further change. In other cases the confusion may need to be demystified and the truth revealed.

Surprisingly often we may not actually know what we are doing. Old habits die hard. Automatic pilot takes over very readily. However, this can never ultimately justify wrong-doing.

New learning is almost always possible. It happens under spiritual guidance according to the nature of the spiritual path being followed. Under the influence of a cynical and unforgiving spirit, for example, all the hurt and bitterness associated with an event are recalled when something similar happens in the future, and this may eventually result in vengeance or litigation. In contrast, under the influence of the Holy Spirit forgiveness is possible and "all things work together for good" (Romans 8:28).

Every conceivable fact of an experience is not usually remembered in total detail because the facts held in the memory are always subject to personal spiritual interpretation. Each of the witnesses of a road accident, for example, usually gives a slightly different account, a different facet of the truth. Total memory of the total truth is known only to God. Biased versions of the truth are held in the memory of other spiritual beings according to their nature and interest.

The memory record of experience which is laid down in the cells of the tissues of someone's body is interpreted by the living spirit of that person according to the spiritual influences who have access to the person. If these physical memory traces are lost through injury or disease, such as Alzheimer's disease, the connection of the memory with the physical body is lost. Although memory for what occurred still exists, in the minds of other people and of other spiritual beings, the individual can no longer connect with it efficiently. Severe physical difficulties then impede further personal change.

Memory is a function of spiritual personalities. God knows the truth about all that has ever occurred (Hebrews 4:13, 1 John 3:20, Revelation 20:12). And although He does not keep the record of sins and wrongs (Psalm 130:3, 1 Corinthians 13:5) God does have access to that record (Hosea 13:12, etc.). It seems most likely that the accuser, Satan, is the one who keeps the record of wrongs and sins, in which case we can assume that memory accords with personality. Thus the accuser remembers accusations. And what is remembered by a spiritual being is what needs to be remembered for the spiritual outworking of that personality according to the character and spiritual allegiances. If the spiritual being has a physical body, such as a human being, the outworking has a physical dimension.

So when we give evidence, and perhaps promise "to speak the truth, the whole truth and nothing but the truth," the truth we speak is how the facts seem to us, without wilful guile, in the light of the god who presides over the justice to which we are accountable. It is only when there is an appeal to the justice of the God of Abraham, Isaac and Jacob in the name of Jesus Christ of Nazareth that the significant aspects of the ultimate truth of the facts may legitimately be expected to become revealed. Even then, the degree of truth perceived will be limited by our imperfect human understanding. However, truth does not depend upon total detail but rather upon the truthful interpretation of occurrences, which is a spiritual function.

Truth and Justice are divine attributes of God, transcending any truth and justice which may be developed through the deliberations of any other temporal or spiritual power. Therefore human memory should not be expected to be absolutely true although it is always capable of change and development in the light of spiritually revealed meaning and significance.

Knowledge

To recapitulate, the remembered meaning of past experiences, and the associated emotional and conceptual connections, form the basis of present behaviour and of new developments in learning and creativity. What has been learned in the past, and how it has been made sense of, determines how we reckon and construe present experience and how we respond to whatever comes our way (Ecclesiastes 1:9). Furthermore, what makes sense, and how it makes sense, depends on whom we have believed in the past and whom we now believe in the present. What we know depends on whom we find credible, and ultimately on whom we wittingly or unwittingly worship.

Our attention is directed and focused and facts are perceived and interpreted according to our personal desires and interests and according to the spiritual influences acting upon us at the time. What we become involved with is automatically reflected upon and connected with our memory and, as time goes on, it becomes spoken about and acted upon in connection with different personal needs and under different personal spiritual influences at different times. In addition, it is imaginatively and creatively used in reflection about other subjects which come to mind at other times. The deductions, thoughts and calculations which occupy the mind as it dwells upon current factual information come from the past but also depend on the present context of personal and spiritual relationships in which they take place. Thus a person's interpretation of facts, their meaning and the use to which they are put, depends upon past and present spiritual influences.

Whatever catches our attention is naturally perceived and enquired into in such a way as to try to make sense of it so that it may be inwardly digested and endowed with meaning. Thus what was unknown and alien to us becomes known and part of us. It becomes part of our personal security and part of the basis for future activity. From what is known we may explore what is unknown. What we have already assimilated has become known to us through the spiritual path we have followed, that is, through the relationships we have found credible and the people, including the spiritual beings, whom we have believed.

When relationships provide security, facts can be made sense of. Security in relationships comes from following a spiritual path which makes sense, which is credible, which figures, which is strong enough to be reckoned with in all circumstances and acted upon with confidence. The nature and adequacy of the spiritual path depends on the spiritual being to whom worship is wittingly or unwittingly given. It also depends on how much personal unhealed experience has had to be hidden. When security in relationship is seriously lacking and there are too many hidden undercurrents which cannot be brought into the light, nothing much may seem to make sense. If confusion should then set in and social rejection should ensue, the mind may become seriously tormented.

Experience does not always follow on in a simple way from what has just recently been going on for us. Quite frequently we are presented with experiences for which we are unprepared, which may startle us severely. Some experiences are shocking and not easy to accept. At such times our insecurities may make us particularly vulnerable. Shocking experiences often take extensive periods of time to be made sense of and to be digested and fully assimilated into our person. Some horrifying events may seem impossible ever to come to terms with. It can seem as though there are holes in the soul or a person may feel shattered "in pieces".

Bad experiences, which have not been healed, naturally engender insecurity and extravagantly bad reactions in consequence. Bad behaviour is the result of bad experiences. Bad events on bad spiritual paths cause more trauma and beget even more trouble.

Through the God who is found through the Lord Jesus Christ of Nazareth it is possible to overcome through all circumstances (Revelation 21:6–7). Jesus went through hell for us and overcame it. No experience is too much for Him. He can take our wretchedness, pain, and horror. He offers healing with peace and love if we will have the courage to turn to him. He wants to save each one of us (1 Timothy 2:4–6).

What do you do when you do not know what to do? What do you do when you can find no one to believe in? You may desperately grasp at straws. You may try to reason your way out of the mess. You may become confused and then become an embarrassment so that other people curse you. This can be a road to madness.

Information is broadcast on the World Wide Web by people under all sorts of spiritual influences in the hope that it may be picked up and assimilated. Many people will grasp at anything which seems to offer information in place of ignorance and confusion. The ultimate purposes of broadcasting such information are spiritual: once a person has caught the bait they may use the information in the way suggested and thus be led to whoever the spiritual being is behind it. There is a battle for influence and persuasion that is directed at our minds. An attractive and interesting path of enquiry is revealed in the hope that it may be chosen by someone for the interpretation of experience. Personal needs and desires may be exploited, regulated or interrupted according to the purposes of spiritual beings. What is accepted by a person, so as to become assimilated, developed and known, ultimately leads to the spiritual being who seeks to be known. Information cannot truly be called knowledge until it has been assimilated and used, so that what is known has actually come to reveal who is known. What really signifies is the name of the god through whom information and knowledge are acquired.

If you try to avoid all spiritual influences and to apply pure reason, the spirit in whom you do it will be your own. When this, solipsism, gets lonely and frustrating the spirit of humanism will be ready to help your reasoning so that when you try to weigh opposing ideas you will find equally powerful arguments on both sides. Eventually you may suspend your judgement. This does not lead to ultimate peace but to ultimate frenzy. Frenzy may actually masquerade as peace but it is the peace of hypnotism, of compromise with powers you cannot overcome, with whom you parley through a frenetic cleverness in your mind so as to take the easy way out. (See Luke 14:32 and 1 Timothy 6:20–21.)

In order to perceive facts rightly it is necessary to have the Spirit of Truth. In order to weigh facts wisely it is necessary to have the Spirit of Justice and to be instructed in the word of God. Whilst the nature of wisdom and righteousness are disputed by those who do not know God, the wisdom and righteousness of God actually bring healing and peace to human beings in spirit, soul and body (Hebrews 12:10–11 and 1 Thessalonians 5:23). Furthermore, He will provide for our needs, if we continue to follow Him, so that we need not worry (Matthew 6:25–34).

Change of mind

The mind of every person becomes made up naturally on surprisingly shaky ground. In view of our unfinished business, unhealed memory, distorted perceptions, frustrated desires and lack of peace with God it is a wonder that we are not destroyed. However, through censoring what causes too much personal anxiety we usually manage to develop a coherence of concepts which gives some integrity to our feelings and behaviour, and upon this we manage to stand and make do. We make decisions and develop purpose into which we willingly direct our energy.

Much of our security is naturally vested in what is socially acceptable rather than what we have personal peace about with God. It is easier to fit in with the other people with whom we live and work than to be personally accountable to God. When we justify our thoughts, feelings and behaviour in the light of socially acceptable reasoning at least we have the security of knowing that other people think the same way and we are not alone. Occasionally God by His grace may wake us up so that we realise more of the truth of what is going on. Sometimes this happens when we are shaken by events.

The insecurity and vulnerability of people is particularly great at times when the interpretation of cultural history is being questioned and when old ways of doing things seem inadequate because of the devastation of wars. At such times the way knowledge and memory have been construed may be personally and collectively questioned and undermined. Much hitherto accepted wisdom may be doubted through having been found wanting.

In view of the need to adapt to new ideas, to political changes, to insecurity at work, and to increasingly complex technology, people commonly look to the political dogma of the state. They also accept guidance from lyrics, drama, journalism and philosophy to give them easy meaning and to help them make up their minds about events. It can be frightening to discover how much the state and the media are able to manipulate mass opinion and control how people think.

Unless the God of Abraham, Isaac and Jacob, the Father of the Lord Jesus Christ is accorded a dignified place of honour in a nation, above that of the state, people may lose their freedom (2 Corinthians 3:17). Otherwise, the place of highest honour within the law to which we are subject will not be that of the only wise God through whom we may live in freedom (Romans 16:25–27).

Fundamental changes can be frightening. Whom can you ultimately trust? When reconsideration and change of mind are forced upon us by social changes which undermine the security we have hitherto placed in collective mythology, the crucial factor is which god we turn to. Whomsoever is called upon will come. Consequently it is necessary to use the proper name of the god to whom you decide to appeal.

Different gods have the power to influence us in different ways according to their nature. They influence the interpretation given to perceived facts, and how those facts are considered and responded to. Different gods alter, in their different ways, the manner in which the mind is made up, and the operation of the censor which excludes anxious thoughts, and the point at which there is the will to act, and the ultimate purpose of each person's response.

The god you choose will probably be the one you find most credible. You will check out the deity with your mind before offering a place of acceptance in your heart because the mind protects and keeps a check on the heart. Once that spiritual being has a place in your heart, the will and the censor and the operation of the mind can be affected more permanently.

Rather than choose a different god for each passing need it is possible to choose the God high over all who knows and loves the heart of every individual and has made it in the image of His own. He has a particular advantage over every other spiritual being in that every hidden secret of the heart may be opened to Him for healing with His love and His peace. God does not give us a spirit of fear but of power and love and sound mind (1 Timothy 1:7 KJV).

He is known through His only begotten Son, the Lord Jesus Christ of Nazareth, who gave His life to redeem us from our sin and who rose victorious from the dead: Jesus gave His life instead of ours so that we might overcome the world, the flesh and the devil and be free. Whoever owes their life to Jesus lives for Jesus. But God is just, so that whoever refuses Jesus walks away from His peace into shaky ground again.

The shaky ground upon which the human mind is naturally made up only becomes firm when the sinful nature is personally turned over to God for healing by accepting Jesus Christ into the heart as Lord, accepting God's forgiveness personally, and then living for Him through the power of the Holy Spirit with all our heart, with all our soul and with all our mind, because He paid that personal price. God will send the Holy Spirit with power into the person who seeks to know Him and follow Him like this. God wants to show us His mind and to reveal it through us; He wants our minds to reflect His and He wants us to do what He is doing. If we remain open to Him, the Holy Spirit will reveal Himself and will draw us closer to Himself, and our minds will change to be more like His (Romans 12:1–3). We remain open to Him by always acknowledging our dependence on Him (Proverbs 3:6) with a meek heart (Matthew 19:14).

The mind changes through revelation. But it does not usually change all at once and Godly change never seems complete in this world. One day things are seen differently, some old ways

A DIAGRAM OF **"MIND"**

MATTER IN HAND

Sensory Functions

Memory

Perception and Discernment

Cognition and Reflection

Imagination and Fantasy

Conceptualisation

Language

Motor Functions

Behavioural Response

Anxiety/Vigilance/ Conscience/Censor/ Awareness

Will

SPIRIT INDWELLING THE HEART

Emotion

Desire

are discarded and behaviour changes. The next day there are new challenges and new changes. If we continue to overcome whatever befalls us though the salvation He offers, He will bring us to His new heaven and new earth where there is no more death or distress. The only firm ground for our pilgrimage is spiritual. God is our rock (Deuteronomy 32:4).

CHAPTER FIVE

EMOTION

Natural emotions

As we all know, babies and little children can be particularly emotional and, since they are so unsophisticated and so open, their earliest development of feelings, thoughts and behaviour must be worthy of special consideration. A healthy baby expresses strong feelings with every new experience and the mother is more or less immediately present with love.

The first thing a newly born baby does is yell into a world that has just dramatically changed through birth out of the womb. The cry is usually met with some sort of acceptance. If the cry should not be received, if there should be nothing in reply, no real meeting, that experience may soon become withering and deadening and the child may lose heart. Usually, however, the child is held, spoken to tenderly, cleaned up and comforted. Child and mother meet in eye contact. As the child's hunger arises it does not immediately connect with the means of satisfaction. But the mother instinctively introduces the teat into the child's mouth and the child sucks, and a little later, the milk eventually comes, with comfort.

With the mother's guidance, the baby comes to know what may be expected. The child's emotional response connects with developing memory that something sufficiently satisfying is usually attainable. Desire becomes more focused. Sense begins the long process of maturation through being tempered with reality and, in consequence, emotions become moderated.

When changes occur, emotions become more exuberant again until sufficient security develops to know those changes are unlikely to be overwhelming. Being left alone for a while may threaten to cause panic until the mother's return may confidently be expected. The introduction of solid food may seem devastating until the child realises that it can be enjoyed. Toilet training can precipitate rebellion and rage until the new comfort is appreciated. The birth of another baby can be the cause of most terrible jealousy until companionship and mutual protectiveness are encouraged to develop.

The healthy drive for satisfaction of developing needs enables a baby to overcome most sensibilities about whatever may threaten to interfere with what is wanted. But for feeding and nurturing to be good enough, some emotion may sometimes seem to have to be swallowed, as it were. Anger about some habitual inconvenience, or fear transmitted to the baby from a frightened mother, or some other naturally generated or acquired emotion, may regularly have to be suppressed automatically by the baby in order for the baby to feed and develop satisfactorily. In order to feed adequately the child has to adapt to the mother. The child instinctively knows that survival depends upon the mother so the child adapts, out of necessity, and this happens at some cost to the child, namely restriction of emotional expression. If such emotions were to be openly expressed to an unacceptable degree they would prevent the baby feeding. No mother need worry too much about this: none of us is perfect. But in this way a child may automatically and habitually come to associate feeding with anger or with fear, or with other emotion that always has to be swallowed when doing it, and the connection may become long-lasting.

This way suppressed emotion may always be present in the child when feeding, although usually it will not be obvious. Unless the child is able to learn differently it may retain the unhelpful association of suppressed emotion with feeding, even into adult life; but by then everyone may have forgotten the origin of the emotional reaction.

Thus, in my case, the personal tendency to bite the hand that feeds me can, indeed, be traced to my earliest days. By the grace of God I have been able to piece together my memories. I have found this incisive tendency to be quite useful for getting into the heart of a matter with determination, which may be why I held onto it for so long. However, I will confess, too, that I have occasionally suffered from painful sores in my mouth, and that both the arthritis in my neck and the associated tinnitus in my ear came from having been stiff-necked with frustration yet stubbornly determined to be satisfied. Furthermore, there have been times when I have had to repent of having comforted my frustrations orally!

Emotions that have been swallowed, hidden away in the dark, or habitually denied, can affect our personalities and the way we think and behave, even though the hidden emotion may not be obvious. And they may even become the cause of illness. This is why John tells us firmly that if we claim to have fellowship with God yet walk in the darkness we lie and do not live by the truth. (1 John 1:6). All the natural reactions about which we have not been open, from the heart, in personal relationship with God, are in the dark so far as our accountability to Him is concerned, whether or not we are aware of them. Because we do not easily take responsibility for them, there are particular problems with those personal reactions that have become hidden from ourselves and about which we are not fully aware. Although we may initially deny their existence, if we develop a relationship with the Holy Spirit, who is the Spirit of Truth, He will enable us, as He renews our minds, to become aware of aspects of ourselves of which we were previously unaware. This is part of the process of repentance into which the Holy Spirit leads us and which continues as we mature in intimate relationship with Him. It requires a humble heart. The more hidden, "dark", material we allow Him to heal in us the more free we become to reflect His nature in the world. Repentance and healing by God's grace make us whole and make us right in our relationship with Him and bring us peace. This process of personal sanctification will continue for the whole of our lives if we are willing.

Awareness of the natural mechanism for hiding emotions and the gradual awareness of the emotions which have been hidden may be embarrassing but may also be used for healing. It can be quite easy to work out the origin of our neuroses, and even of our physical illnesses, once we realise the truth of how our personalities and characters have developed and matured. The Holy Spirit will show us what to confess and will lead us into healing if we listen to Him and allow Him to affect us and change us.

Although I had the best mother in the world, I have had to forgive her for having refused to feed me on demand when I was a baby, and for having, in the nicest possible way, been so dominating and controlling. I have had to do serious battle with demons of frustration and impatience and I still have a weakness in this area, which I have to guard against. This is why Jesus says if your mouth (or whatever) offends you, cut it out (Matthew 5:29–30). Well, you cannot cut your mouth out, but you can cut out from your life pathways that lead you into trouble and, furthermore, God can heal the whole problem provided you obey what he is saying. It is those natural reactions which are not in right relationship with Him, and which are thus not admitted to the light of His truth, which have to be confessed to Him, so that we may be free to receive His healing.

Every baby would have been as frustrated as I was if faced with the same problem! But I have had to confess that I was sinful to have held on to my frustration and I have renounced that frustration and have accepted God's forgiveness and healing in the name of Jesus. Because Jesus shed His blood to save me, I can forgive my mother and have no further need, metaphorically speaking, to draw blood from her or from any other mother-figure who tries to feed me, or from any matter (very similar to "mater" which is Latin for "mother"!) which I may find frustrating. In short, I have no longer any need to bite the hand that feeds me.

Because my mother did not make right with God the process of feeding me when I was a baby, I have had to make it right with God myself. If she had recognised my frustration as a baby, and had taken it seriously, and had allowed herself to be affected by it, and had thus openly taken responsibility for her response to it in relation to God, the frustration would not have remained stuck in my soul for so long. Unless our natural reactions are satisfactorily met with God's transforming truth and blessing, they will need healing. Human nature can only avoid its own destructiveness by divine redemption.

Emotions are spiritual

Emotion is the response of the human spirit, manifest through the soul and body, to what is going on and what involves the person. The emotional expression will be influenced by various other spiritual influences affecting the person. Thus, emotions are the natural responses of the soul to all the relationships in which the person has become involved. They include our needs and desires for food, excretion, air, security, sexual activity, understanding, shelter, rest, and so on, as well as our fear, anger, envy, shame, rejection, and all our other natural responses. They are the raw, rudimentary replies to what is going on and they come from the awakening touch and the consequent movement of the heart and mind. They enable us to connect with our whole being to reality, and thus to engage with what is real.

If our emotions are denied we lose contact with reality and may go mad. Emotion is a component of behaviour which is both a spiritual and also a physical manifestation of personality.

Emotions are never mad. If they should be treated as unworthy of consideration, part of the individual being would be denied an opportunity to come into the light. Although they may be sinful (as was my frustration) they are not naturally wrong in themselves. They may be inappropriate, as when my habitual frustration when feeding in later life made me feel frustrated when sitting down to a very adequate and leisurely meal in pleasant company. However, all emotion can be understood when human nature is understood. Moreover, emotional responses can be changed through open, truthful, loving relationships and they can be healed through openly intimate relationship with the Holy Spirit. The mind and emotions of a person reconciled to God, and at peace with Him, express His mind and emotions for that person's situation.

When we become aware of some emotion or feeling, it may be named in common language. The natural account we give through our language bestows different names on different feelings and emotions, according to human nature. Different languages have different words for the same emotions and feelings and the words of the language come from the heart (Matthew 15:18, etc.). By and large similar sorts of situation will produce similar natural emotional responses in all human beings. Various spiritual influences and social controls give cultural nuances to expressions of emotion. However, the Holy Spirit has the power to cut through culture and bring alive truth.

Emotions are stronger than feelings: whereas emotions are felt in the heart with some power, feelings could be said to derive from educated sensitivity and sometimes they may be rather indistinct, as when we say, "I have a feeling which I cannot quite make out." Thus we could say generally that it is necessary to have emotions in order to connect with reality and to have feelings in order to be discerning.

At a meeting with a stranger, the soul naturally responds to the other individual, who is as yet unknown, with alertness and with a readiness either to withdraw from the encounter or to defend the self. The third possibility, of course, is that some openness each to the other might become possible so that there may be some personal meeting. To meet in a spirit in which there may be concord would enable the guard to be relaxed somewhat. It would relieve the defensive tension. Then it could become possible for each to allow into the heart the spirit of the other to some extent, for each to affect the other in complex and subtle ways which would lead to beginning to know each other and to the beginnings of sentient relationship. Otherwise, the automatic, defensive preparation for flight or fight will be maintained, although this is often disguised with some sort of formal mannerisms or politeness.

Both negative withdrawal, in some degree of fear, and also positive opposition, with some degree of aggressiveness, are associated with a physiological increase in the production of adrenalin and other hormones. The biochemical effect of these hormones increases the state of alertness of the body and also the state of readiness of the body's physiological self-protective and healing mechanisms so as to be able to cope with any trauma. However, although hormones alter with emotions, it is not necessary to assume either that every emotion is mediated by a different hormonal response or that hormones are the cause of emotions.

The biochemistry of the difference between hatred and jealousy, for example, has never been discovered and even if the day should come when biochemical differences between the various emotions are revealed, the fact will remain that hatred and jealousy and fear and anger, and so on, are essentially different spiritual influences. Whilst different emotions are associated with different behaviour, they are spiritual phenomena, the product of our spiritual nature.

All spiritual beings, whether they have bodies or not, express emotion, and the preponderance of expression accords with the nature with which God created them. Wasps may become angry, and dogs may become jealous, and piranha fish are notably voracious. Butterflies seem happy. Similarly, spiritual beings preponderantly manifest particular emotions according to their nature. Thus it may be discerned that Satan operates through pride and fear and the Holy Spirit brings love and peace. There are many spirits of fear, many spirits of cruelty, confusion, control, insecurity, and so on, and some of them have the names of pagan gods, and there is much deception to disguise their true nature. The Bible promises that the day will come when all creatures with bodies in this world will be spiritually transformed so as to live together peacefully (Isaiah 11, Romans 8:19–21) and that another day will come when all spiritual beings, both with and without physical bodies, whose names are not written in the book of life, as judged by God, will be consigned to eternal destruction (Revelation 20 – 21). The power for redemptive change rests with God.

Meanwhile, there is for us a path of life and immortality (Psalm 16:11, Proverbs 12:28) which can only be discerned accurately through intimacy with the Lord Jesus Christ of Nazareth. There is also a path leading to death and destruction. It is through living in relationship with Jesus, through allowing the Holy Spirit to be lord of the soul, that our natural emotions and feelings may be transformed onto the path of life instead of leading us to destruction. We confess our emotion to Him, and we yield it to Him. He holds us in love so that we do not retaliate according to the human spirit of our fallen nature, although we still feel and have emotion. Although we may have to use our willpower to overcome with Him at first, the longer and closer we live with Him the easier it becomes.

Emotions drive the thoughts and the will. What is felt affects and is processed by thought: by imagination, cognition, censorship, conceptualisation and language. And there are checks and balances, involving memory and reflection, so that human beings do not generally respond with emotion that is raw and uncontrolled. Emotional expression in human beings has many variables and enormous complexity. Thus there is a reciprocal relationship between the emotion of the heart and the functioning of the mind.

Our spiritual allegiance, the spiritual person who is our lord at any given moment, determines our interpretation of experience and the censorship of our behavioural responses. All sorts of beings may try to entrance and control us, particularly when we are vulnerable. Whoever is credible, whoever figures, may be allowed to have influence in the heart and whoever influences the heart affects the mind. So it matters whom we worship. The Holy Spirit is the one who gives freedom and peace.

Extremes

Unless emotion is openly, adequately and personally met it may naturally become uncontrolled and cause harm both to self and to others. Unmet emotion is a natural cry into a void, yelling human passion that can terrify, famously depicted in Edvard Munch's painting called *The Scream*. Not only may it wound the personal soul but it may also strive to dominate and control other people until there can be some social accounting. Damage may be extensive unless personal self-control is allowed to develop.

In the early, formative years a baby learns to cope with most emotional responses through always being met by the mother and by other familiar people on whom it has proved sufficiently possible to depend. The baby's emotions may be extreme but the child is naturally receptive to learning, particularly because separation from the mother occurs only slowly. A mother instinctively distinguishes her baby's emotions, and knows whether the cry means the child is hungry or angry or frustrated or uncomfortable, and so on. Long before the child can speak words there is mutual spiritual discernment and knowledge. She naturally

makes appropriate responses from her spirit and heart which
serve to contain the child's emotion by making sense. The sense
and context of the mother is imparted to the baby and the individual child naturally grows more separate from the mother as
a sufficiently secure base of sense and knowledge is being
acquired. Through playing and through imitation and through
dreaming, experience of emotional response and how it is met
is incorporated into a body of substantial meaning that coheres
through nuances held in common with familiar people. The
development of a child's emotional intelligence depends on
comprehensive interaction with the mother and the father in
safe-enough space, with a variety of things that may be used
playfully so that learnng may be gentle. Thus emotions are generally contained by common sense. Even in adult life, however,
we need frequently to take time to allow our emotions to
proceed into playful reflections so that understanding and
embodied knowledge and appropriate responses may develop.

Sooner or later, however, calamity strikes and the resulting
emotion in the child often seems devastating. It is quite
common for there to be episodes of constant and frequent
crying for which no cause can immediately be found. They are
usually precipitated by some failure of communication, or
some lack, the precise nature of which is lost to everyone.
Temper tantrums are common, too. When the crying or the
temper seem unrelenting the possibility of meeting and con-
taining the emotion in a way that is easily acceptable to the child
seems to disappear. When the containment of the emotion
through any mutually sentient meeting seems impossible, in
order to prevent harm it is necessary to hold the child quite
firmly with love for as long as it takes for the crying or temper
to subside. Then the child will eventually feel safe enough for
the passion to be peaceably subdued.

There are other calamities, too. Accidents, disasters, serious
physical injury, overwhelming violence, difficult relationships
that result in despair, neglect and abandonment, all produce

heart-rending grief and terror, rage, rejection and hopelessness. Such passions are natural in such circumstances and it would be callous for a child not to feel them; but only rarely can they adequately be met or held with truth and love at the time. Consequently, they frequently leave wounds in the soul like spiritual ulcers, black holes that remain super-sensitive to the emotion which caused them. Then whenever that same emotion is naturally aroused in the future its expression may be excessive and it may trigger memories of the original trauma. Thus, until healing is found for the wound, the soul remains vulnerable to particular issues and inclined to seem unreasonable. Furthermore, a lasting sense of woundedness and hurt may easily beget a sense of injustice and bitterness with a sense of rejection, through seeming different, leading to rebellion and a set of beliefs and affiliations which may easily develop during the formative years into intolerance and prejudice. In all sorts of ways this may militate against personal peace.

Demons easily attach themselves to such wounds and use those areas of the personality that are vulnerable and sensitive to wreak further subtle destruction. Only just now I have read in my newspaper of the sentencing of a murderer who claimed to have no recollection of the crime. He was known to have attempted a similar murder previously. Many serious crimes are committed by people who were suddenly overcome by a passion because demons had entered their souls through old wounds.

Thus unhealed wounds may cause periodic trouble to erupt, sometimes with serious damage. Occasionally the power of their passions can horrify, panic or confuse both self and others. Often the existence of woundedness and demonisation, and even wrongdoing, is denied for shame, or for fear of rejection. Those then remain latent causes of lack of self-control, shame, criminality, madness or illness until they are allowed to be exposed to the light in a space where the demons can be expelled and the wounds healed with the truthful, loving authority of Jesus. He has the power to meet and to hold the most damaged people, and to heal them, even though they may sometimes fear that they could disintegrate if ever they were to begin to let go of their overriding passion. Indeed that very passion may sometimes seem like the only thing to give meaning to life.

After a person has grown big and strong it is more difficult than it is with small children to meet them or to hold them in extreme emotional distress. The hope is always that emotional self-control will have developed with maturity. Any real meeting of distressing emotion in adults depends upon mutual willingness to try to be truthfully accountable and upon an atmosphere of hospitality toward human failing, with empathy rather than sympathy. Unless each person carries their own load (Galatians 6:5) external controls may have to be imposed. Then it will be necessary to use spiritual authority.

When self-control has been lost, and a person is overcome with powerful mixed emotions and associated thoughts and demons, which may be confusing, they may sometimes be said to be out of their mind. If the willingness to take responsibility for oneself and to be careful with other people has been lost, the disturbing person may, for their own safety and for the safety of others, find themselves in a situation where they can only be held chemically, with drugs, or in some other sort of prison. In this case the nature of the restraint imposes restrictions on relationship which may sometimes hinder the spiritual work of healing.

Nevertheless, such restraint can provide some sense of safety. A person may be relieved to feel held together with drugs, in hospital or even in prison sometimes. There are other means, too, for blanking out from awareness stimuli that threaten to produce uncontrolled or intolerable feelings and reactions. Some people hold themselves together at the expense of others with constantly aggressive behaviour or some other assumed attitude. Loud music, particularly if it incorporates lyrics giving vicarious voice to the overriding emotion, also sometimes seems to serve to hold a person together. Some people shut themselves away in isolation for the same reason.

Disguise

When thoughts, feelings or behaviour seem intolerable there are drugs, for those who want them, to make a person feel better or think differently or behave in a way that is not so distressing. It may often seem easier to take a drug from a physician than to bother to get to the root of the trouble, especially if you seem unable to afford time and space for reflection because it is necessary for you to go to work to earn enough money to pay for food and shelter and all the things you have to do for the people you care for.

There are many people who are out of touch with their bodies, their minds and their true feelings because they seem to have to ignore themselves in order to keep going. Furthermore, the spiritual atmosphere in the home, in the workplace, in the clinic and (most sadly of all) in the church is not always conducive to the exposure of any weakness or to the distress of opening old wounds, with their seemingly irrational emotions and thoughts, or to the admission of sins requiring forgiveness and healing. When the Spirit of God is quenched (1 Thessalonians 5:19) it may be necessary to put on a face in order to cope.

There are often natural social sanctions against those who reveal any inability to cope, unless they should be deemed worthy recipients of charity. Charity is a word which used to mean Godly love of one's neighbour but which has been modernised, since the industrial revolution, to mean a disguised form of pity by which empathy is avoided. It is a brutal fact of human nature that those who betray a weakness may become the butt of condescension and may even be exploited and abused because of it. Furthermore, it can be dangerous to feel true compassion for someone who cannot cope, and to allow oneself truly to understand, because such empathy can sometimes arouse unhealed wounds, sensitivities and emotions in oneself and render oneself vulnerable in a similar way. So it is common to try to stop disclosure of unhealed emotion because others' knowledge of it could cause us to be exploited, too.

There is a stronger resistance against facing the truth about their human failings in people who never had a father whom they could love and respect because he loved them in their weakness when they were young. Many such people are far too exasperated with anyone in authority ever to believe it may be safe to be true to themselves (Ephesians 6:4) or that it may be possible to be met and held together lovingly without being abused in any way. Bad experiences with earthly fathers can hinder relationship with our loving Father God. Avoidance of Him, and of the truth He allows to be revealed, creates stresses that cause illness and lack of peace. But God wants to turn the hearts of fathers to their children and the hearts of children to their fathers in forgiveness (Malachi 4:6 and Luke 1:17).

There is an automatic mechanism of censorship that suppresses and stops the disclosure of thoughts and feelings that produce too much anxiety and insecurity. So when much of what is in the heart cannot be said openly, a feeling of sadness may arise within oneself because so much of one's own personal truth has to be disguised and kept hidden. A sense of self-rejection may develop, and a sense of shame, and these, too, will be hidden. The person may find it difficult or impossible to be aware of the origin of these feelings and demons will readily exploit the distress in order to make the hidden trouble more permanent and destructive.

It is far more common than is generally realised for a person to have been very severely traumatised and confused at some time in their life, often in their childhood. Many people are able to put on an acceptable face to disguise the way they really feel inside for most of the time so that it becomes easy to deny, even to themselves, the truth of what happened years ago until some event triggers the confused memory and the buried emotions and threatens alarming disturbance. Sometimes the mechanism of censorship will struggle to repress awareness of it all to such an extent that a person can feel they exist only in their mind, disconnected from their body, and they may have so-called "out of body experiences". Sometimes the censorship mechanism may be under such extreme stress as to cause a person to seem disconnected from part of their total personality, so that when their circumstances change their inner disturbance becomes controlled by the censorship mechanism in a different way so that their personality seems to change. Demons use such states of being to wreak more havoc and destruction so that it can seem extraordinarily difficult to unravel the damage.

We cannot get to the root of these sorts of troubles purely through logic. We may try to find logical explanations for how we feel but, by itself, our logical reasoning produces only defensive justification and practical ways for coping. Justification may be turned into law and legalism but without repentance there is no true healing. Logic offers no personal meeting and unburdening of the heart in the loving, forgiving, holding, healing presence of Father God. Faced only with the accuser and the facts, repentance and healing do not occur.

Our natural need to be able to make sufficient sense of what seems to be going on to make up our minds and take whatever action seems necessary to keep on going often causes us to close our minds to deeper exploration of personal issues. We naturally like to bring closure and to escape from uncomfortable issues as quickly as possible. The exigencies of everyday life often seem to leave little time for reflection even at the best of times, let alone when there is deep distress. Even prayer times often become perfunctory. Provided we seem to be behaving in the same way as most other people we can seem to have adequate self-control and be content to seem to be coping from day to day.

Culture and Law

Cultural mores may disguise and cover up all sorts of hidden issues in a whole population. Artistic expression of one sort or another proclaims and indulges common emotional sensibilities and secrets so that people may be given a sense that their hidden and buried emotions and thoughts are not so peculiar after all because other people have similar emotions and thoughts too. Identification with the reaction of other people to what is portrayed in drama, painting, music, and so on, may give a person a primitive sense of identity within a society. Although we may derive some comfort from the vicarious expression of what is hidden in our souls, it does not bring any true healing

Sadly, the laws of most nations reflect much of what is socially acceptable as right and wrong whilst failing to acknowledge that justice has any divine authority. Although "You shall not murder" (Exodus 20:13) may indeed stop murders by divine authority the fact that such law is effective in regulating emotional expression in society is only rarely attributed to God these days. There is an increasingly respected body of legal opinion which argues that in view of the natural inclination of a majority of people to react to particular events in particular ways, such as to react with fear to violence or with disgust and shame to various sexual offences, new laws should be so framed as to protect the sensibilities of the majority.

Laws prevent emotions from progressing out of control so as to cause serious offence in much the same way as totems in animistic cultures. The totem is an image of a presiding deity, who is not to be offended, which strikes enough fear into the people to be effective. For those peoples who choose to ignore the existence of spiritual beings, the letter of the law must be spelled out whilst the presiding deity remains hidden.

Thus, instead of being met or held, many natural emotional responses are disguised or suppressed or censored by the individual, under pressure of persuasion from social attitudes learned from the very earliest years, backed by law. The sciences of medicine, psychology and sociology, taught and studied in academic institutions that are generally humanistic, uphold the commonly accepted social and legal values through systems of classification and thought which ignore divine revelation in order not to offend the common sensibilities of intellectuals who do not know how sinners can be saved. However, the word of God through Paul is that we should not rebel against governing authorities (Romans 13) but that we should remain free from personal bondage (verse 8) keeping Jesus as our king.

To step outside cultural norms can be frightening and confusing even when you are Christian. The sense of identity is threatened. Some unsaved people who end up beyond the pale act mad in order to gain the benefits of a little charity. If ever you should become to some extent socially excluded it is best to seek the guidance of the Holy Spirit, whom you meet through the Lord Jesus Christ of Nazareth. He will meet you, hold you and provide for you in such a way that you will not be subject to the judgement of any human being (1 Corinthians 2:15–16). Jesus died outside the city gate to make people holy through His own blood (Hebrews 13:12–14).

Politics

I was recently asked by a mature Christian lady whether or not it was necessary to visit the doctor for antidepressants or some psychology because it did not seem possible easily to stop weeping. She feared that real mental illness may be setting in. Past events previously hidden in the family had come to light and there was suddenly serious trouble, particularly amongst family members who were not so used to keeping short accounts with God, and it was all threatening to get out of hand.

If emotion is suppressed, by drugs etc., so as not to be consciously acknowledged and admitted to the light, there will be some degree of failure to take account of all that is going on so that people may fail to know where they truly stand one with another. Emotional responses to events help us to make sense of the details of our personal involvement in the world. When emotion is denied, despite being present in the soul, there is deception and there may also be confusion. Emotions not openly owned and expressed may manipulate, dominate or control other people because those other people are denied the chance of addressing those emotions openly. If they realise this is happening they may become seriously offended.

If other people fear the expression of emotion, the whole situation needs to be brought before the Lord. Fear of others' emotion may have been learned in childhood but it may prevent a person from easily making sense of events. On the other hand strong emotion can indeed sometimes be most terrifying and Christians need to know the authority they have as children of God (John 1:12) in order to bind and loose (Matthew 18:18) and overcome in such situations.

Suppressed or denied feelings not admitted to the light may create an atmosphere more obvious to others than to whoever is causing it. And such an atmosphere may be difficult to understand and may cause people to feel troubled, resentful, guilty, and so on. Through their natural responses to the atmosphere people can be manipulated. This is the essence of sorcery. Whether or not the atmosphere is created knowingly the full truth of its nature may sometimes remain stubbornly obscure.

It usually helps if everyone involved can admit how it makes them feel because the effect of the atmosphere tells a lot about it. If the true nature of the atmosphere can be clarified peace and healing can come. Ultimately the word or words that capture its essence are given by revelation. This is most likely to come if the Holy Spirit, who is the Spirit of truth, is actively invoked in the name of Jesus.

Often people do not know what they are doing when they create an atmosphere. The atmosphere may, in truth, have more relevance to unresolved issues from a person's past than to anything going on in the present. But an individual may not be able to put words to what has always been hidden or denied (as was the case at first with my personal frustration connected with feeding, previously described). Getting to the nature of the emotion and the associated thoughts will first of all involve admitting there is an issue to be healed, that is a general move of repentance. Then as the Holy Spirit does His work what has been hidden, forgotten, suppressed, denied, may slowly come to light, often at first through pre-lingual processes in the mind and soul. Thus playing, drawing, music, creative work and crafts may be more expressive than words. Other people may begin to tell their story using words that are more powerful and significant to the teller than the hearer. Some may use poetry. A process evolves whereby the actual emotions and the connected issues are eventually named adequately for a true account to be given to other people and to God. This process may need help and encouragement. Occasionally the faithful help of a professional psychotherapist or counsellor can be useful. When all the issues are put right with God He gives His peace and healing. God's Spirit of truth enables clear words to yield sense by which we may find our way with His peace (Psalm 119:105).

What matters is to get in touch with the feeling, to express the emotion and to feel the implications of it, rather than to indulge it so as to allow the devil a foothold. Once something is expressed it is actually easier to do it next time. But to suppress or deny the truth of emotion that is within you is deceptive and perpetuates stress. Once it is expressed you can give an honest account. There is no need to attempt total emotional catharsis because only the blood of Jesus can purify you so as to bring peace (1 John 1:7).

You tell Him how you feel and you put it right with Him. We are told to be rid not of everything negative but rather of malice, deceit, hypocrisy, envy, slander (1 Peter 2:1–3). You confess what you naturally feel and think, you renounce what He indicates, you receive His healing into your body and soul and you do what He gives you.

When we are walking clear, unhindered by hidden emotions and their concealed thoughts, we are free to speak and act from the heart without guile (John 1:47) without spending too much energy consciously calculating everything.

When a person is firmly in God's will there is peace; but to pretend to have this peace by acting a part, as some people do when, in truth, it is not really present, can be dreadfully deceptive. When a person is walking clear God may use that person's emotional responsiveness to express His feelings about a situation. God uses the whole alive person and He does not expect us to be zombies. When we die to our old self, to our fallen human nature, we become free to live fully and emotionally for Him. Jesus wept (Luke 19:41 and John 11:35), Jesus was in anguish (Luke 22:44), Jesus was thankful (Matthew 26:26), Jesus became angry (Mark 3:5).

Jesus lived with us in this world and He knows what it is like. In His love and truth God is always willing to meet people with compassion and patience just where they are (1 Timothy 1:15–16) when they accept Jesus. He suffers with us (Hebrews 2:5–18). He is generous and merciful and eternally faithful (2 Timothy 2:11–13). His love endures for ever (Psalm 136). He brings people who listen to Him and treat Him seriously into a spacious place of salvation (Psalm 18:19) and He sets the lonely in families (Psalm 68:6). Furthermore He is the God of peace who can turn our wailing into dancing (Psalm 30:11).

He is the perfect Father who really loves us people and knows every detail of our mess and longs to heal us gently (Psalm 139; Exodus 15:26) so there is no need to try to hide it from Him. He made us in His own image and has the same feelings and emotions as we do, except that there is nothing in Him of fear (1 John 4:18) or of death (1 Corinthians 15:54–56) and His thoughts are way beyond our understanding (Romans

11:33–34) and He is not encumbered by the needs of a physical body in this world.

It is both what we hide through fear, and also what we become involved in that could cause our natural emotional responses to progress to death, that will always be tending to drive us into depression or madness or illness. God allows us to suffer in this world, and He grieves with us, so that we may seek Him and know His saving grace. When we turn to Him through Jesus our personalities change as He saves us.

Our human emotions will in fact always be met by some power greater than us. It is up to us whom we allow ourselves to meet. If we really know who He is we can go to Jesus. Or we can go to some worldly group or institution composed of other people. Or we can go to the devil. If you find you are not adequately held by other people, the devil will try hard to get a hold of you unless you turn to Jesus. For this reason churches need to learn to be hospitable communities able to meet those who are rejected by the world. If relationships are lovingly, truthfully, patiently maintained, the Holy Spirit will use the various talents of the people drawn together into Jesus for the development of the fruits of the Spirit, including self-control and soundness of mind (Galatians 5:23, 2 Timothy 1:7 KJV).

CHAPTER SIX

SEX

Physical intercourse

Our sexuality is particularly fascinating because it may involve us in most exquisite intimacy, most profound passion and most beautiful pleasure privately with someone of the other sex.

God made men and women different and complementary (Genesis 2:20–25) and He told husband and wife not to deprive each other of their pleasure in each other's bodies (1 Corinthians 7:4–5).

At peace in a safe place, coming together in love with commitment each to the other and consent easily given, modesty is gradually shed with developing interest and enjoyment of each other's bodies. Entrance is given to hidden places of soul and body. You marry. Each becomes known to the other to the extent of becoming one in flesh. This intimate celebration needs no accessories; everything that gets in the way of physically opening to each other and joining together is laid aside. Pleasure focuses in the genitals together. Orgasm is a shared peak of glory, a climax of mutual worship, a declaration of love absolutely affirmed in the possibility of pregnancy.

The Bible says your body does not belong to you alone but also to the person to whom you are married (1 Corinthians 7:4) so each has a duty to help the other to orgasm because orgasm is important for mutual pleasure, satisfaction and cohesion. It is best taken fairly slowly for too much excitement can spoil it. Orgasm comes with mutual openness and with unity in spirit; and the best spirit in which to find unity is love. With time you get into delightful ways of enjoying each other this way.

Sexual enjoyment helps by the grace of God to keep couples together even when times are hard or relationships are difficult. Even at moments when all love seems to be lost, if sexual pleasures are still shared they may help enormously to keep a marriage intact. So sex helps in the rearing of children in more ways than one. Not only does it enable us to beget children but also it helps the father and mother to stay together through thick and thin in order to provide a sufficiently-secure environment to nurture them into maturity. This is how God made us and it is good.

To embark on this journey lightly, however, without regard for the consequences, is extremely foolish. To be willing and able truthfully to lay aside all your considerations and sensibilities and resistances, and to open your heart and body to another person without shrewd commitment, is dangerously reckless. If ever you imagine that you can just give your body, without your heart or mind being both involved and affected, you will be mistaken.

It is, of course, quite possible to deny the feelings in your heart and to cut yourself off from them to the extent that you are unaware of them. This involves hardening your heart so that it becomes calloused. But your heart is part of your body and affects your mind and is involved in all you do, whether you like the fact or not. Although you may be able to censor the memory of what you have done with your body, and all that it means, from your conscious mind, the memory remains, even though hidden. It may suddenly come to the surface of awareness without warning if you are reminded by similar circumstances. It may also be brought to conscious awareness by the Spirit of God working in you. Then you may suddenly be horrified by all the implications which you never allowed yourself to know about before. Then you realise that you have retained emotions, memories, influences, that connect you with the other people with whom you were intimate, which you had never before realised. These connections may not always be nice. They represent unfinished business that it is naturally impossible to sort out unless you have remained committed in soul and body to whomsoever you were sexually intimate with. Only when your heart is reconciled with God by accepting Jesus in repentance is it possible to receive His forgiveness and healing and to break the bondages of your soul. Then you discover a peace of heart you did not know before.

The only sure way to avoid this sort of confusion is to be married, by coming together before God, so that commitment one to the other may be ratified through solemn vows, knowing that God will hold you to those vows, not by force but through withdrawal of His blessing if they are broken. Mutual commitment then becomes a covenant of marriage, with the solemn promise that the two lives are laid down each for the other before God. This creates adequate security for openness together, for growth in maturity together and for the rearing of children.

We people are not just bodies, nor are we machines. Relationships can never be only physical. Relationships always involve the whole of our being, spirit, soul and body, whether we want to believe this or not. When two people come together physically, there will ultimately be a fundamental disharmony that can eventually lead to intolerable stresses unless there is spiritual agreement in worship. But when God is worshipped together in the name of Jesus, and taken seriously, the love and knowledge of each other's different souls and bodies can be worked out with real joy together, and always with healing.

This is why sexual sin is described in the Bible as mortal (Romans 1:27, 1 Corinthians 6:18). Sexual sins that are hidden from the light of God, and never put right with Him, bring an element of disharmony into future physical intimacy. The resulting stresses can become the cause of illness.

Furthermore, if we should choose not to be accountable to God for all we do and say in this life and for all our relationships, we can be sure we shall be so after we have passed through death.

God is always in it

Liaisons which are known to be forbidden by God naturally cause guilt and shame. Nevertheless, knowledge that certain sexual relationships are wrong may add a piquancy to them and the consequent excitement and adrenalin can easily become addictive. Fantasy may take the place of reality to stimulate the addiction more. Then it becomes difficult to recognise the guilt and shame that secretly drive the lust for further forbidden sexual pleasures.

Our human nature is naturally rebellious. We can tell when we are justifying ourselves rebelliously, and making untruthful excuses for illicit desire, through the thrill of excitement that accompanies the pursuit of lust. The devil uses the adrenalin of our rebellion to deceive us into believing that excitement is necessary for sexual pleasure. However, the truth is that excitement spoils it because adrenalin makes people hard and wounding rather than sensitive and receptive.

When sexual relations are conducted according to our maker's instructions there is rest for the heart and general blessing because the pleasure is joyful and good, home is fortified and families are held together in love. The God of peace wants the peace of Christ to rule in our hearts and homes (Colossians 3:15). If we relinquish lust and turn to Him in repentance we may know the joy of His healing consolation. His joy comes with peace (Proverbs 12:20, Psalm 94:19).

Adrenalin is the hormone produced in the body when the natural reaction is to fight or to flee, which is a state of excitement. Such excitement is a state which naturally precedes real meeting in some spirit of concord. Addiction to adrenalin is popular, perhaps because peace and security are so rare. Adrenalin addiction is so popular that it is commonly assumed that in order to enjoy something you need to be excited. So entertainment is contrived to be exciting and to stimulate our adrenalin through fantasy.

However, this sort of entertainment should be distinguished from true enjoyment. If you continue to pursue an activity whilst the adrenalin is flowing it may give you "kicks" but you will miss the joy that God wants you to know in all you do (see 1 Peter 2:11). The thrill of the chase may be the pride of youth (1 Samuel 17:34–37) and many older people cultivate it, too, through striving to stay tough, but macho behaviour can wreck ordinary relationships. It is personally insensitive and defensive and there is no real peace in it.

It is a sad fact that medical and psychological scientific terminology adds to our confusion about this by describing sexual "excitement" as a natural concomitant of sexual enjoyment. The word "excitement" is in truth being used by them as a technical term to indicate physiological changes found when particular emotions and nerves are aroused. Mechanistic scientific language distorts truth if it is transposed unconditionally into the language of relationships. Although some excitement may be essential for romance, it is not true that the excitement of adrenalin is necessary for sexual enjoyment. Nor is it true that more real enjoyment is produced by more excitement.

Whatever we run after, and whatever we indulge in with trepidation, may stimulate excitement so that the thrills seem to provide us with relief from boredom and take the mind off misery. Such temptation can be hard to refuse, particularly in childhood, when a person is at a loss for interest and eager for new experience. Doing naughty things, including naughty sexual things, is often accepted as an inevitable feature of growing up. But those of us who are given the privilege of helping other people find healing for their souls and bodies know that habitual and addictive patterns of behaviour may eventually develop into serious sickness; and the trouble will often be found to have started in the naughty excitements of childhood.

The only way to avert such danger is to be able to talk intimately but openly about everything, including secrets, with your children before about the age of ten, before they are too old for the wounds inflicted in the world to have made them too defensive. This can be done by asking what they think and by entering into easy playful discussion with them without any absolute demand that they must hold the same opinions as yourself. Unless they feel able to retain their own free will they can easily feel oppressed and in this way their exasperation may develop into rebellion (Ephesians 6:4). When strict commands or prohibitions are given they often act as the focus of temptation (Romans 7:8) and, because of our rebellious nature, they readily serve the cause of the development of secret sin. Nevertheless there is no need to withhold from your children the wisdom you have learned through your own experience, nor to deprive them of knowing what you believe to be right and wrong. Nor can it ever be wrong most strictly to prohibit imminent danger.

Children accept wise guidance when plenty of time is spent with them in an attentive but unobtrusive way, allowing them to be openly accountable in such a way as to make it easy for you to reply in ways they accept. It involves faithfully earning their respect and allowing them to love you, not rejecting their love no matter how disguised it may sometimes be. It involves loving them unconditionally and never abusing them. If there are subjects, like sexuality, which you are not at peace about within yourself this will be apparent to the children, so it is best to have sorted out your own heart and mind, with God's help, before you have frequent involvement with them.

Things which are naughty are done in secret but a child does not naturally have secrets. In fact, it is natural for a child to be entirely open about every aspect of life with those people who are intimately trusted. Secrets develop from learning to be defensive and having experiences and thoughts that seem too dangerous to speak about at home. A child learns to have secrets when taboos are discovered and when it becomes apparent that certain subjects should not be openly discussed because of other people's extreme reactions.

This is not to say that a child should have no private life; but rather that a child should be respected as a separate person and be encouraged to develop individual thoughts openly without anyone else dominating or controlling the mind. "Where the Spirit of the Lord is there is freedom" (2 Corinthians 3:17).

Of course, there are aspects of sexual relationships that are private. The particular intimacy in which one person opens vulnerably to another in sexual intercourse cannot be shared with other people without risk of serious wounds. Children cannot be expected to comprehend all the essential nuances. Nevertheless, sufficient explanations to satisfy them can be found, and there is no need to deny that sexual intercourse takes place. The sooner they learn the rudiments of how it happens, and that mother and father enjoy it, the better; but it would be far too intrusive for everyone concerned to permit them to observe it. In my opinion the age at which most children are ready to know about sexual matters from parents is when they ask, which is often between five and seven although not necessarily so. If sex education is only given at school there will be the risk of making it too exciting as children play with the information with each other. And it is foolish to fuel mutual interest in sexual intimacy amongst adolescents. This way many children may become sexually promiscuous because the checks and balances from peers and teachers can never be as personally meaningful and effective as those found at home amongst parents and brothers and sisters.

Children have to learn also that parental love can be given to others as well as to themselves without possessiveness and without any loss of love or security. Young children, as their independence increases, gradually learn to be able to let go of their mother but they may become naturally jealous if their mother shows love to another person, whether it be a sibling or husband or anyone else. When mother and father kiss in the presence of the young child, the child will often try to get between them; but through being gently pushed away the child can learn that there is no option but to allow mother and father to belong to each other in a physical way and have some sexual privacy. Parental guilt about this will make a child's frustration worse. But when the child knows that firm exclusion from the sexual intimacy of mother and father will always be imposed, the child will naturally become content, accepting love without sex. Interest in sexual intimacy will then only reappear naturally after adolescence. Thus, when the child eventually falls in love, natural restraints will be in place, learned from the parents.

However, the devil has ways of messing up children's lives for his own destructive purposes. If a few children in a particular locality have somehow or other become accustomed to some secret sexual addictions, others easily covertly join them. It is difficult for a child to tell parents about something which the child knows will distress the parents greatly, which could get many other people into trouble, and which could also result in ostracism from the child's wider peer group. If the parents are known to have had secret sexual habits of their own, such as adultery or addiction to pornography, the child may even believe it to be normal to have some secret sexual addiction or other.

In this way sexual demons spread amongst children and remain secret. Pornography and sexual fantasy, masturbation and mutual masturbation, homosexual and heterosexual promiscuity both with other children and with adults, are surprisingly common around adolescence. Although the children may imagine that these habits could be stopped at any time, an inner compulsion to continue them will often have developed, which cannot, in fact, be controlled by the will. This is not only done through the actual sexual seduction of children but also through subtle propaganda in the media, through suggestive lyrics, stories and pictures. Even though there may be a strong desire to escape from the compulsion, like a hunting dog hungry for food the child will return to the lust again and again. And these habits often persist into adult life and interfere with marriage and social relationships.

Such sexual habits, lusts and addictions may be found to have been introduced into the locality at some time or other in the past through incestuous families. Any adults who may currently perpetrate them will often have been infected through other adults in their own childhood in the same sort of way as they infect a new generation. They compulsively seek the companionship of children and groom them for it to become possible to introduce sexual adventure as something naughty but nice that can be shared for excitement and pleasure. Sexual propaganda from adult media is easily made available to children to make precocious sexual activity seem grown up and acceptable and thus infect them with addictive lust. Grossly explicit pornography is generally easy to acquire and it waters the seeds of abomination in the name of freedom of speech.

This sort of behaviour may be indigenous in various pagan families and societies. But where Jesus is known as Lord and the Holy Spirit is active the sin becomes apparent. This can cause disguised hatred and persecution – and subtle seduction – to be directed towards Christian families.

Lusts may sometimes be inherited. A demon in a parent causing a craving for fornication or for homosexuality, or whatever, may be passed down to a child and be manifested spontaneously as the child gets older. Then the child may be under the illusion that the powerful tendency cannot be healed because it has been inherited in the genes.

Jesus can set people free from these things. First, He must be met and accepted as saviour and a personal commitment made to Him. Then the sin is brought to light and fully confessed and renounced. Then the feelings, ties and bondages with the other people involved in the sin are clarified and then renounced and broken and reconciled to God. Those people are forgiven. Then personal forgiveness is received in the name of Jesus. Then any demons are systematically expelled in Jesus' name. People really change and find permanent healing through being reconciled to God this way.

Politics

It is easy, however, to become frustrated and secretive about our sexual desire unless we negotiate our relationships with adequate regard to the truth of it. Although a surprisingly large number of people have the gift of celibacy, the vast majority of us do not. In order to live in contentment with our own sexuality, in such a way as to have lasting health and peace, it is necessary to be accountable to God for the individual sexual nature we seem to have.

If we should choose to rebel against God and to be accountable only to mankind, anything goes these days. This might sound interesting until you have the gumption to realise that most people are so enchanted by the joys of uninhibited sex that they turn a blind eye to all the trouble it causes. Furthermore many Christians mistakenly believe that sexual immorality should not be spoken about[1]. However, the people worth listening to are those whose eyes God has opened to the true enormity of all the trouble caused by doing whatever you

---

[1] Ephesians 5:11–12 should be translated: "Have nothing to do with the fruit-less deeds of darkness, but rather expose them. For it is shameful to mention *in secret* what the disobedient do", instead of ". . . what the disobedient do in secret".

fancy. They are often people who know because they have really suffered in consequence of their own mistakes or the mistakes of others close to them. May God give them the courage to talk more so that God's saving grace may be more widely known!

After having been healed in the name of Jesus from any uncontrolled lustfulness or inherited or acquired sexual sin a person will be left with the sexuality God intends. If ever any doubt remains it is possible these days to determine your sexuality genetically. Occasionally genetic investigation and counselling may put you in an unusual genetic category so that your attempts to fit the common social stereotypes become confusing. Or it may reveal unusual sexual vulnerability, or the impossibility of having children. Such conditions may be hard to bear. God's word in such circumstances is: "I love you as you are. Take courage. Be content with what you have. Never will I leave you; never will I forsake you." (Hebrews 13:5; Philippians 4:11–12).

Sexuality becomes increasingly obvious and defined in the years immediately following puberty, at a time when a person is usually too immature to provide adequately for the children which would naturally come from ordinary sexual intercourse. Restraint is natural, provided adolescent teenagers have been accustomed to being easily accountable to elders they respect, provided they are not tantalised by grossly sexually provocative material and provided sexual demons have not been introduced to make aspects of their sexuality uncontrollable. Restraint does not mean that sexuality is hidden, rather that there is a natural awareness of the consequences of lack of restraint which can enable the person to behave responsibly. To encourage loosening of such restraints before marriage is extremely foolhardy.

Tantalising sexual imagery, however, is so ubiquitous in many societies that sexual temptations are hard to resist. Our imaginations have the capacity to form images of what we desire which appear so vivid and detailed that we may be drawn powerfully towards our lust. Many people know how to present themselves in a charming way so as effectively to manipulate us into being fascinated by them. Thus we may often come under the spell of an apparently attractive person and behave in ways we may later regret. And when our desire is sinful indulging in fantasy about it can drive us powerfully further into the sin. Added power is given if we are addicted to the adrenalin of being excited by what is naughty. This is the essence of pornography. And it has been discovered that the thrill of sexual fantasy can be associated with all sorts of products in such a way as to enhance sales. Sexual excitement may be introduced into literature and drama to sell a message through books and films. A person's potential to stimulate other people's sexual fantasies can often determine whether or not someone gets and keeps a job. Sexual fantasy is so much part of life that there is a general demand for its evocation in most social situations. Many people have become so used to sexual fantasy that they are unaware of being powerfully manipulated by it.

In this atmosphere, is easy to indulge in various sexual fantasies for enjoyment of the excitement followed by the release of the frustration the fantasy generated, especially when a person is lonely or sad. Fantasy is often associated with masturbation, which provides physical sexual excitement followed by release, albeit solitary, and therefore providing only an unreal, virtual solution for the sadness, loneliness or frustration. Self-stimulation increases the propensity for fantasy and thereby increases fears about reality. Furthermore, when a situation similar to the fantasy actually appears in reality, the fantasy may be enacted with undue excitement as all self-control is overpowered. The fantasy is enacted as if it were appropriate to the true reality, which can increase social anxieties alarmingly by making the individual seem foolish after the event.

A young man who had always lacked confidence due to family turmoil and lack of encouragement developed hatred for a pretty woman with whom he had had a brief affair. This girl not only jilted him but she also stole from him and mocked his prowess publicly. When he used to masturbate she would come into his dreams and he developed fantasies of retaliatory sexual violence towards her which he rather enjoyed because it gave some semblance of release for some of his frustrations. Later, after taking another similarly pretty girl home from a nightclub, he found himself in a rather familar situation when she rejected his sexual advances. His response was to attack her and rape her. As it happens, he caught a serious sexually-transmitted disease from her and he is now serving a long sentence in prison.

In this and similar ways sexual fantasy is deceptively a most potent destructive force in society. It destroys marriages, renders children insecure and begets disease, abuse and crime. It causes bonds of interpersonal goodwill in society to be fractured, contributing significantly to the fragmentation and destabilisation of society.

When there is devastating war, and faith is undermined, what was once believed to be right with God is fundamentally questioned as if nothing in the past had worked. People cease to believe that it is better to have loved and lost than never to have loved at all. And when war and its aftermath have made many people profoundly distressed and insecure they are easily tempted to comfort themselves sexually, in order to escape from the pain of reality, without considering the need for commitment. Sexual fantasy can be all the more prevalent and destructive at such times. Rational arguments are made about how harmless and enjoyable it can be. Its subtle destructiveness is not taken seriously because even the leaders of society indulge in it. Since contraceptives make it possible to have sex without pregnancy their use becomes an excuse for promiscuity. Abortion is made available for unwanted pregnancy without any regard for the severe emotional suffering it causes. Groups advocating homosexuality receive public money and campaign amongst disaffected people for the destruction of the conventional family. Feminist groups celebrate the liberation of women from the home. Legislation to control immorality seems impossible to impose because it could be threateningly unpopular.

Sadly, the connection between human wretchedness and addictive sexual immorality is largely denied by academics. Some varieties of the distress it causes can be academically classified as illness without the aetiology being extended into moral or spiritual or even social fields. Medicine does not recognise any relationship between anxiety or depression or obsession and sin. Since technologically sophisticated medication is expected to be effective there is no need to think further. In the absence of a strong church standing dignified in the word of God, government relies on academic argument. So, in the absence of spiritual succour that is adequate to the truth of human wretchedness in all its forms, the temptation to run after fantasies can easily be overwhelming.

It is the god who is worshipped who ultimately determines the expression of sexuality (Romans 1:18–32). It is the god who is honoured nationally who ultimately determines the prosperity or wretchedness of a people (Exodus 20:4–6).

Certainly there would be less wretchedness if we could stop abortion. Everyone who comes openly and truthfully before God after going through an abortion sooner or later makes confession of real devastation. Any intentional taking of human life is surely murder. Wittingly or unwittingly it generates shame.

Perhaps there would be less devastation of human life, too, if we were to rid ourselves of contraception but in this very imperfect world it seems necessary for sexual relations to be enjoyed without pregnancy for the sake of family stability. It should be noted however that pagan families seem to be growing at a faster rate than Christian. There is less risk of the actual fertilisation of an egg by a sperm, and consequently of taking a human life, if barrier methods of contraception are used, such as condoms, rather than hormonal methods which, although they inhibit ovulation, can sometimes work through preventing implantation after actual fertilisation.

Shame

In cultures where sexual fantasy and paganism are endemic (and this includes most cultures, not just the sophisticated western cultures in which sexuality is blatant and promiscuity is flaunted in the media) almost everyone will, to some degree, have been seduced and manipulated by sexual fantasy, at various times in their lives, against their better judgement and therefore to their shame. They will have become the pawns of the fantasies of other people and they will have been misled by their own fantasy. The extent of the consequential damage, and of the unfinished business unwittingly incurred, may be horrendous. Opening the eyes to it can make you feel caught in a sort of spider's web.

There was a woman who had been taken into mental hospital suddenly without warning many years ago, when she was fourteen, and who had lived the rest of her life in psychiatric care. Although she had never seemed, on the face of things, to be ill, on getting to know her better it could be seen that she was sexually promiscuous, apparently without much self-control. There seemed to be nothing unusual about her family. Her brother, now an old man, said he had never had any idea why she had been taken away in her youth. But now that he had time to think about the past it was beginning to trouble him. "They just took her," he said. Only very recently was it revealed to him by another sibling that their father had had incestuous sexual relations with that daughter when she was a small child. In consequence, from the time of puberty she had been permanently distressed and had subsequently grown rather confused, although she was usually able to cover up her instability very well. But by now both the mother and the father had died.

Nevertheless, the extended family still lived with the shame and, unless there is healing for it, future generations will to some extent live with it too.

Very commonly, it is more difficult to be frank about one's sexuality than about any other subject. This is the source of the shame naturally connected with it. One's past and present sexual desire, fantasies, activity, relationships and sexual secrets can often account for an awful lot of trouble, both personal and social. In societies where sexual mores are less restricted and there is more promiscuity, as seems to have been the case in ancient Greece, the shame is disguised by various forms of pride. The pride is sustained by putting down particular categories of people, such as slaves, or assuming dominating superiority through manipulation, politics or violence. Political correctness at the behest of a controlling regime will thus always hide a multitude of sins.

In your family and amongst the people who trust you, in the church and in places where you are well known, it would be too embarrassing to reveal the extent to which you have been promiscuous and unfaithful sexually, if only through fantasy (Matthew 5:28), or to reveal the extent to which you have been sexually seduced or abused. Whom can you trust to keep such confidences? Few people have dealt with their own souls before God sufficiently to be personally disinterested when told disturbing secrets about others' lives. There are very few people who can be trusted to handle very sensitive confidences with integrity.

Sexual secrets very readily become a favourite subject of gossip. Words may slip out inadvertently and word spreads, often inaccurately, about what people are supposed to have been doing. And so a person may be avoided by others, and treated with some suspicion and fear, and respect may be withdrawn. Damaging judgements are often made after a person has been desperate for healing but unable to find it due to other people's ignorance and prejudice.

Shame is the natural reaction to secret sexual lust and to the personal damage that results from it. But shame is generally too powerful an emotion for anyone to allow into conscious awareness. If put on the spot, a person will usually become angry or violent rather than admit to it. Without Jesus shame is usually totally denied so that a person will not even be aware of it. Shame can only be confessed and faced when there is a way out. It can only be overcome by giving it to Jesus because "the Lord has laid on Him the iniquity of us all" (Isaiah 53:6).

It can be easier to be open about your personal sexuality in a non-judgemental atmosphere, such as a specialist psychotherapeutic group, where you know everyone else has similar faults, where you have no lasting attachment to anyone and where there is no chance of blackmail. But such environments are hard to find. The weakness of such groups can be that the shame is so common and so powerful that the culture in which it is shared collectively becomes a culture in which shame is the norm. Then later it may it become apparent that the shame remains, like a pall, to blight a person's life. Although all the shame can be declared, it is not truly overcome because it is not confessed to God as sin and His healing is not accepted through Jesus, who became shame instead of us (Hebrews 12:2) so that we may be released from it.

Even though there may be confession and renunciation of wrongdoing, even though confusion may be untangled and natural emotional reactions expressed and understood, even though serious secrets may be brought to light so that they cease to drive an individual to repeat them, even though there may be forgiveness, and even though the soul may feel free thereby of much of the burden of guilt, there still remains the curse of shame until we let the Lord Jesus Christ of Nazareth set us free.

As soon as we truly receive Jesus we become aware of our human unworthiness. In truth, it is not only people guilty of sexual depravities who feel shame but also people guilty of any sin at all. We all feel shame if we try to approach God, no matter what precisely we may be guilty of, because we are human and our nature is fallen. It is important and significant to be able to feel it. It is only when we know and accept that Jesus shed His blood to save us that we find confidence really to enter God's presence (Hebrews 10:19).

Everyone can feel condemned but there is no need to be condemned – not even the very worst offender (Romans 8:1–2). When we accept Jesus and receive the Holy Spirit, it becomes possible to see that shame is a gift from God to lead us into repentance and into reliance on nothing and no one but Him for salvation. Jesus will take our shame away, if we yield it to Him, because He became shame for us when He died on the cross (Matthew 27:35–46 and Hebrews 12:2). He overcame it when He rose from the dead.

Furthermore, if we yield our hearts to Him with all of our sin, He will freely give us His Spirit if we ask. He will enable us to break the ties of guilt and obligation and unforgiveness and all the other emotions and ways of thinking that bind us to other people and restrict our freedom of relationship. He loves us unconditionally. His shed blood redeems us. This is a supernatural gift freely given to those who turn to Him in faith. We do not need to be good, nor do we have to justify ourselves. We must allow the Lord Jesus Christ of Nazareth to be our only righteousness. We only have to confess our sinfulness to Him and ask for forgiveness and healing and He will come to us and enable us to be willing to forgive others, even those who abused us badly. He will help us to try to do so even when we do not feel like it. Then God can, and will, forgive us so that all our wounds may be healed ("by His wounds we are healed" Isaiah 53:5). It can be just as if we had never sinned (Romans 5:9). This way we are, for real, set free.

It is usually necessary to have the help of two or three other Christians in private to sort out such issues, often over a period of several months or years, people who can keep confidences, who are not staggered by how really bad sin can be, who can survive despite all the bad thoughts and feelings which arise in you as your secrets are revealed, and who are well versed in the authority of the word of God. Such people usually work in pairs: Jesus sent His disciples out two by two (Luke 10:1). Folk like this will have known the Lord's healing themselves in order to be able to minister His healing to others.

CHAPTER SEVEN

HUMAN NATURE

The trouble

Although we like to think we are good, there is not much evidence for it. But if ever we should be accused of being evil it is always far too much for us to bear and always creates very angry opposition.

People say, "You are what you make of yourself. There is good in everyone." And when someone does something bad or crazy they say, "There must be something wrong with him. He needs professional help." Bad or crazy behaviour is commonly considered to be a sign of illness rather than a spiritual condition. And it is commonly assumed that illness is an affliction whose origin is adequately known to the professionals. But it is not commonly realised that the professional help usually only involves attempts to suppress the symptoms with drugs, and sometimes with psychological manipulation, because it is not considered orthodox for professionals to address spiritual matters.

When something goes wrong people ask, "Why isn't more being done to stop this sort of thing?" And they say, "This sort of thing must never happen again. Someone must admit

responsibility and take the blame." As though it is the professionals who should have all the answers these days.

In this sort of way we assume that as rational human beings
collectively we should really be able to handle everything this
world can throw at us. Thus it is assumed that our natural love,
the love by which a parent nurtures a child and cares for those
who belong, must be good and powerful enough to be extended
into sufficient goodwill to make the world a better place. It is
assumed that we should naturally be able to be truthful and
considerate at all times. It is assumed that our education should
be able sufficiently to expand the information and abilities
available to us, that our psychology should be able to instruct
us how to behave and get what we want, and that our medical
services should be able to tell us how to avoid being ill and
should always be able to fix us when disease strikes. It is
assumed that humanism can harness the human spirit to
science and democracy in order to bring peace and make our
culture abundantly successful. And this way we tacitly assume
that we have no need for God's divine wisdom.

However, despite our best intentions things continue to go
wrong. People do things that are bad or crazy, they make mistakes without really meaning to do so, and their best-laid plans
fail to avert trouble. The whole body of education, science and
politics fails to avert war, famine and disease.

In order to delude ourselves that the solutions to the problems
of the world fall within the scope of human endeavour, we
human beings automatically censor what we see because true
reality is too horrendous, too painful and too oppressive without
a divine saviour. It is characteristic of fallen human nature to
shut down the sensory apparatus to the full realisation of what
seems to be unbearable and to close the eyes to the full extent of
human wretchedness and depravity (Psalm 107:42). To begin to
open the eyes to the ubiquitous suffering of humankind, the
destruction, the torment, the killing, the starvation, the ravages
of illnesses, the oppression, the endless suffering all over the

earth, is to begin to realise that it is all far too great for there ever to be any serious hope of a human solution. This is not to accuse people of being inherently evil but to indicate that whatever good is in us, and whatever we make of ourselves, may have power to care and to cope and to create temporary cures but does not have power to heal. Human beings cannot redeem themselves out of corruption. No politics, and no technology, can be soberly imagined to be adequate to heal it. The God of Abraham, Isaac and Jacob, with whom Jesus enables us to have intimacy and to know as Father, is the only God mighty enough to encompass it all and the only God to be able to save us. Without God's grace and mercy there is no health in us (Psalm 38).

Sin

It only becomes possible to open the eyes to the real extent of human wretchedness when you know Jesus, because He gives adequate hope of salvation that proves to be real. "While we were still sinners Christ died for us" (see Romans 5:6–8). Faith for salvation really is possible because of what He did on the cross and because of what He has continued to do in the lives of those who know Him personally. Through Jesus hope becomes credible and faith has substance. This in itself is proof of His real victory.

Until you know Him you can feel condemned at the very idea that human nature may be sinful and even at the very mention of the word "sin", which militates against any peaceful and sober consideration of it. Sin cannot properly be considered in the abstract; it is too powerful a concept (John 3:20).

The word sin refers to the absence of redemptive qualities in our actions and reason. Because we are naturally sinful, by nature we oppose God unless we remain in relationship with him through willing submission to His Spirit, whom we receive through Jesus. Our natural reactions are sinful, whether or not we know what we are doing. Human sin is natural.

When the Holy Spirit of Jesus is present with power, both the human nature and the demons of a person may react to Him because He challenges them (see Mark 1:23–24, John 13:6, Acts 8:7, etc.). Thus the Holy Spirit makes our sinful nature apparent. People may do and say things they seem unable fully to control. When the Spirit of God moves us into repentance, however, we can find freedom and healing. The ultimate fruit of the Holy Spirit living and working to make us right with God is joy with peace (Galatians 5:22) and freedom (2 Corinthians 5:17). So we can only bear to see that we are evil (Luke 11:13) when we really know that Jesus will save us and continue to save us. We know this when we meet Him.

Then our natural reactions and responses to what occurs in our everyday lives need constantly to be transformed by His Spirit, and harnessed to the personal gifts He gives us, in order to bring the power of God's supernatural healing into our individual lives and thus into the societies in which we live. This way, disciples of Jesus are salt and light in the world (Matthew 5:13–16).

The health of our best-laid plans depends on whether or not the spirit in which they are made is that of God. He gives wisdom to those people who willingly belong to Him and if they seek His face He speaks to them through words of knowledge and prophecy so that they may know something of His mind (Isaiah 42:9, Amos 3:7 and 4:13). But although we may be part of His plan we cannot know His whole mind (Isaiah 40:13). All we can do is purify ourselves by availing ourselves of His healing in order that we may always respond obediently to His Spirit. When we are submitted to the Holy Spirit living in us, our responses are becoming those of the Holy Spirit so that we come to feel what God feels. Our anger, for example, can be His anger if we are perfectly right with Him. Although we are human and have our freedom, our reactions and responses may, by the grace of God, have a righteous quality and we may reveal His presence in the world through our lives.

So we may put His will into effect and play our part in bringing about His eternal purposes.

The Bible relates, in Genesis 1 and 2, that God created human beings to guard and protect His garden, and to rule over every living creature, but that we fell from the grace of an innocent relationship with God by being seduced by Satan into eating from the tree of knowledge of good and evil, which God had forbidden. This was rebellion against Him. Because of it we died in spirit by losing our connection with His Spirit of eternal life. Thus we became aware of our exposure and vulnerability and lost the special guidance and protection of living closely with God. We were banished from His garden to a life of toil and pain and death in this world. But God continued to love us, and He kept His hand on us, and He accepted the sacrifice of the lifeblood of animals when people called to Him. He heard them because they acknowledged that lifeblood was the price which had to be paid for our return to Him, because we had scorned His life and the life is in the blood (Leviticus 17:11). He replied to their animal sacrifices and established His law amongst them so that they might know how to live in order to find His life. But we have not been able to obey His law because we have never seemed to have had the spiritual strength to do so. Nevertheless, He loves us with such jealousy (Isaiah 7:14) that He conceived by His Spirit a Son by a righteous virgin called Mary. This only begotten Son of God, Jesus, submitted to becoming a sacrifice for us. On the cross He allowed His own lifeblood to be shed for us, and died, so that those who believe in Him might be saved and have eternal life (John 3:5, 16). The same Holy Spirit who raised Him from the dead not only enables us to believe but also is available to empower us to be free to do what God is doing, to overcome the human nature we were born with, and to overcome the powers of this world and of the devil, in order to do the work we were made for, namely to guard and protect His garden, His kingdom, and to feed His sheep.

After you have accepted Jesus and received baptism in Holy Spirit (1 Corinthians 2:14–16) you will usually find you are able to understand the logic of human nature much better than you did before. By growing in the love of God and of your neighbour your empathy increases and your prejudices are destroyed according to the direction of the Holy Spirit. The mistakes and confusions of this world come to make sense when seen God's way (John 9:39–41). But although natural human reactions may, by the grace of God, be able to be understood and seen as reasonable and logical this does not thereby make them justifiable or endue them with goodness.

Natural, sinful living, without being reborn in the Spirit, leads continuously to unresolved results. It chronically affects our physical bodies, tending to cause sickness, and spoils our relationships, tending to cause trouble.

When you are seeing in God's way can you see our fallen nature for what it is (1 Corinthians 2:14–16). In the light of God, our natural reactions and responses without the Holy Spirit are seen to be expedient rather than healing. They obey the third law of motion, discovered by Galileo and enunciated by Newton, namely: "For every action there is an equal and opposite reaction." They naturally retaliate. For everything that impacts us there is naturally an equivalent response according to human nature. Thus we have a natural sense of justice.

Talion

This principle of equity has been used in law from time immemorial to make the punishment fit the crime. Action and equivalent reaction give us a sense of reasonableness. The exaction of condign punishment for wrong done satisfies the natural need for recompense. Because it brings civic peace, talion (or, response in kind) has been a basis of law worldwide for many centuries, and it was perfected in the law given by God to Moses. The principle applies to natural human behaviour in general. If something is done to me, I am not naturally satisfied until I make a sufficient response in kind.

If you are frightened there will always be some reason why but, regardless of the reason, it may well be entirely logical for me to try to control you in response; if I control you, it may well be entirely logical for you to become resentful; if you get resentful, I may logically become angry; if I get angry, you may reasonably become stubborn; if you become stubborn, I may logically mock; if I mock, you may logically despair; if you despair, I may logically hate you; if I hate you, you may logically reject me and feel violent towards me. If self-control is lacking or weakened, in the absence of divine forgiveness, rejection and violence may result.

I say such reactions are logical because they are understandable. They are understandable and seem reasonable because our human nature enables us to empathise with them; that is, if I put myself in the other person's shoes I know I could naturally feel what the other person feels and may respond or retaliate as the other person has responded or retaliated. However, it does not follow that such reactions are justifiable or good. In themselves they have no healing or redemptive power. They ultimately result in fear and bitterness.

For relationships to be credibly genuine, however, this quality of natural understanding must be present. On this basis, and despite cultural differences, people who meet from different parts of the world can fairly easily sense whether or not their relationships are authentic. The human spirit causes individuals to respond in ways that are universally recognizable.

Furthermore, the quality of self-control is also universally recognizable. You can usually tell if a person you meet is using a lot of willpower to suppress emotion. When the responses that come naturally cause too much anxiety they are censored and automatically not allowed into conscious awareness and not translated into action (as described in Chapter Three). But what is censored in this way nevertheless becomes a hidden motivating factor that exerts a powerful effect on a person's demeanour. You can usually tell if someone is driven by trouble hidden deep in the soul.

You can naturally tell, too, whether or not someone's spirit is reconciled to God and truly at peace in what they are doing. The emotions, behaviour and language that emanate from another soul naturally cause equivalent retaliatory responses and understanding. And if you know the peace of God through Jesus you can discern the truth of the apparent peace in someone else (John 3:6) that is you can discern their spirit. But without the self-control over your own natural reactions that comes from the Holy Spirit you could sometimes be intimidated, dominated, manipulated, or even controlled by another person, through being deceived. Some people develop the craft of producing natural responses in others in order to gain power over others. In fact this is the essence of witchcraft.

Seriously calloused people, thoroughly used to deception, sometimes called psychopaths, may have a remarkable ability to deceive other people, by automatically denying their own hidden emotions and affecting the demeanour calculated to manipulate, dominate and control other people for their own ends.

Demonic beings also take advantage of our natural human responses to manipulate our behaviour and self-control, if they can. They are more likely to do this if we are wounded, or if our wills are dominated by other people, or if we allow ourselves to be misguided through doing things we know to be wrong. Demons may come to live in us symbiotically as spiritual parasites. They may seem to be so very useful at the time that we are actually glad of their power, and believe we need them, and allow ourselves to forget what it is like to be free. Our natural fear, for example, may enable us to avoid a dangerous, recurring situation and these circumstances may be used by a demon of fear to make us subject to fear which becomes uncontrollable and which progresses so as to make us terrified in many social situations. So the demon can do a lot of damage by dominating the mind and emotion and by controlling situations. This sort of thing may happen easily if we fail to discern demonic influence in our personal life and if we fail to take authority over it and expel it in the name of Jesus.

Furthermore, it is easy to imagine situations like this in which taking a sedative may seem like an advantage, by calming the nerves. Then a demon of addiction may take advantage of those circumstances to make it seem impossible to face the world without the sedative. In this way we lose our adaptability, our reactions acquire an uncontrollably compulsive urgency and we become controlled by our need for sedatives: we automatically organise our lives so that they are always available.

Thus the naturally retaliatory responses to experience, past and present, which may occasionally be demonised, habitually determine the behaviour of the natural person.

However, Jesus can liberate us from the constraints of retaliatory behaviour. By having borne in His own person on the cross the full impact of corrupt human reaction and response, and by having risen the third day victorious from the grave, Jesus gives us healing. By His wounds we are healed (Isaiah 53). "The punishment that brought us peace was upon Him" "so that we might die to sin and live for righteousness" (1 Peter 2:24). Through Jesus it is possible to forgive and be forgiven and to exercise the authority of a child of God over the temptations of this world, over our human nature and over demons. So Jesus heals the personality and changes human nature.

Offence and blame

It takes both courage and a living relationship with God not to judge or condemn someone who has caused offence but rather to be able to say, "I forgive you. There but for the grace of God go I!" Those who have never accepted Jesus usually stop a long way short of saying this because to see themselves as similar sinners is unbearable if they know no saviour. The anxiety of considering it triggers their censor and they retaliate.

A follower of the Lord Jesus will be enabled by His Spirit to resist an evil person and, if struck on the cheek, to turn the other cheek. If sued a disciple will be empowered to give whatever it costs and more – with the proviso that it is best settle matters quickly so as not to let an issue come to court (Matthew 5:25 and 38–48). A true Christian will love an enemy and pray for a persecutor. Jesus paid the price for us so that we no longer need to take serious offence and so that we may be set free from the natural law of sin and death (Romans 8:2).

Nevertheless, Christians do not live in a perfect world and, even in Christian societies, trouble occurs to show Christian disciples how they need to change in order to be closer to Jesus and to prove that Christian behaviour comes only from our personal relationship with Him. God wants us to know for sure that His kingdom, where He is truly king in each individual heart, can never be established by law, through being controlled legalistically, but only through the power given by lives laid down for Him in love.

At present, however, law based in the principles of talion and equity, with provision for the prevailing system of rights and obligations, brings relative but imperfect peace and stability to diverse societies and nations. Provision has to be made for different systems of rights and obligations because different spiritual influences create different sensibilities that may cause offence to be taken for different reasons. Consequently, in different cultures civil peace may be disturbed in different ways and justice is demanded for different things in different ways.

In Romans 13, Paul tells Christians to obey the established authorities wherever they live and to refrain from political rebellion. The kingdom of God will come " 'Not by might nor by power, but by my Spirit,' says the Lord Almighty" (Zechariah 4:6).

However, just laws backed up by the means of enforcing them

are not, in themselves, totally sufficient for the maintenance of civic peace. Unrest may particularly break out through grievance at complaints seeming to be inadequately met. Religious disagreements occur because demonic spiritual powers challenge each other and always challenge Jesus. The cultural climate is determined by prevailing spiritual authorities. Effective peace does not come from satisfying a majority but rather through Godly principles of justice becoming acceptable to the hearts of enough people of sufficient influence and credibility in a society, so that the natural forces of rebellion are overcome. In this unhealed world where people's hearts are often troubled, the practical exercise of spiritual authority remains the most necessary foundation for effective law.

Compulsive repetition

When you do not have much peace about something that has happened you are left with a persistent sense of unease that does not go away until greater peace can be obtained. There may be a sense of injustice. There may grief or anxiety. There may be very powerful emotions. When you give voice to your complaint you may be authoritatively overruled, sometimes in very subtle ways. When others do not accept what you say you may not be able to make sense of other people's responses. Then you are likely to be left with an impression that no one will meet you, or hear you properly, or take you seriously. You may become confused or even quite paranoid.

When this has been the case, you may decide that you need to modify what you say in order to compromise so that someone may begin to help. Then there will be aspects of what you personally experienced, and of what it meant to you, and what you think and feel, which you suppress. Although what happened may have created hidden resentment, you may adjust your account and deny the resentment, for example, to take cognizance of prevailing attitudes and save yourself from ostracism.

This may become automatic. You may become unable to admit to or to speak openly about the facts as you have truly perceived them. You may even begin to doubt your own perception.

The natural censorship mechanism automatically shuts off awareness of thoughts, memories, and imaginations that would otherwise create intolerable anxiety through being misconstrued or rejected if they were brought out into the open. To bring them to light may seem to threaten you with intolerable consequences. When things happen which cannot be fully made sense of, or sufficiently responded to so as to bring satisfaction and personal peace, they are unconsciously kept on hold in the memory with a remaining desire for satisfactory resolution, for peace and for healing.

This sort of thing happens both to non-Christians and to Christians alike. Christians only have the advantage of knowing that Jesus can eventually heal them if they allow the Holy Spirit to take over, which is not always easy.

Then whenever a set of circumstance arises that reminds the individual of what is buried in this way in the memory, the individual automatically responds in such a way as to try to get peace for the old memory. In one way or another events are re-enacted so as to provide some possibility of making sense of what happened, and of finding peace and healing. Sometimes the trigger is emotional and so emotion is remembered, even though the memories connected with it are not, and a lot of deep emotion may be expressed for which the reason may not be immediately obvious. Alternatively, people sometimes find it uncanny to have arrived back in the same sort of situation they have always been avoiding.

History repeats itself, as they say. This happens not only to individuals but also to whole societies. Issues put out of mind, or dealt with by inadequate legislation, will keep coming back until the peace of God is found for them. These sorts of issues can only truly be heard and met and made sense of and overcome by Jesus: His loving, truthful, healing presence is necessary to sort them out. His Holy Spirit of wisdom and understanding and counsel and power and knowledge and of delight in the fear of God is necessary (Isaiah 11:2–3) for good personal and public government.

Thus after an horrific road accident in which major injuries were sustained and several people were killed, which left him with both physical scars and unbearable guilt, the man responsible was unable to tell all that happened or express all the emotions for fear of compromising himself or falling to pieces. A severe prison sentence eventually more or less satisfied relatives of the victims, so he thought he had paid the price for his mistakes so that he could put it all behind him. But he suffered nightmares and would frequently awaken terrified. For a long time his soul had been unable to find peace and forgiveness about it all. Then a similar incident was portrayed on a film he was watching on television. He suddenly wept and started to shake without immediately understanding why. But he was in sympathetic company and friends realised the film had reminded him of the accident. They helped him make better sense of what had happened. He poured out his guilt and sorrow. One of them was a Christian who showed him how to accept Jesus. He accepted that Jesus paid the price for his sin and took his guilt and shame. He forgave others and received God's forgiveness. From that moment on his nightmares stopped and he found healing.

According to our human nature, those events that are not satisfactorily resolved are all unconsciously stored in the memory until something causes them to be remembered. Sometimes they may make us ill until something happens to enable us to connect our illness with buried memory. God made us this way because He loves us and wants us healed through Jesus. Remembering (or re-connecting) like this, is a sure sign of the hand of God on our lives, repeatedly offering us the chance of healing. Without really knowing what we are doing, we go back to events until we find peace about them. We may sometimes even find ourselves inadvertently returning to places connected with forgotten but unhealed events. When we get old we naturally think back over old memories again and again and this is really in an attempt to get peace about them before we die.

A woman who could never forgive her father for having walked out on the family, leaving her and her mother destitute when she was a child, was never able to trust any man ever again. In consequence she drove one husband after another to despair. Such was her reserve, suspicion and unforgiveness that each one left her. So the pattern of the original wound repeated itself. When told about Jesus she refused to forgive. She died of a cancer in the stomach. People knew her cancer was connected with her bitterness but sadly her stubbornness and pride were never overcome.

It is the censorship mechanism that determines the nature of the peace we settle for. Another word for it is the conscience. It is under spiritual influence. Whatever god we worship and whatever demons we hold on to will determine what we believe to be right for us, and what sort of anxiety and how much anxiety we are prepared to live with.

The Bible calls the God of Abraham, Isaac and Jacob the Father of the Lord Jesus Christ and "The God of peace" and speaks of the peace of God which transcends all understanding and can guard our hearts and minds in Christ Jesus (Philippians 4:7). A peace of protective power and life-giving intensity, greater than any other peace, may be known by those who accept Jesus. When a person's censor, or conscience, is ruled by the indwelling presence of this peace, that person gets free and the eyes will perceive truthfully, the ears will hear with understanding, the heart will respond with wisdom, behaviour will be righteous, authority will be given (John 1:12) and healing will come (Isaiah 6:9–10).

One way or another the truth of our past catches up with us. If we do not succeed in bringing it to God in the name of Jesus and in finding His peace and healing, it may become a hidden force that causes trouble, it may be the cause of torment, and it may make us ill. Furthermore, if we do not settle these matters with God through Jesus in this world we shall have to account for our natural reactions face to face with Him, and receive His judgement, in the next (see Ecclesiastes 3:15).

Once, when I was taking a psychotherapeutic group in a jail, with long-term prisoners convicted of very serious offences, one of the men asked why, after having himself experienced the pain and torment of having been most cruelly sexually abused as a child, he should not have learned from the experience so as never to inflict torture like that on any other human being.

Prisons and psychiatric clinics are places where unspeakable things can sometimes be revealed. Although it is difficult and uncommon for people in such institutions to be disinterestedly listened to, such listening can be instructive. You find that what people have ended up doing is often similar to what was done to them. How they have behaved and thought, even if it has been called sick or given a diagnosis, can be seen to have been a logical consequence of their personal experience, according to their human nature and demons. People who have not known loving fathers often have not themselves made good fathers and so their children may have looked for love and truth elsewhere and may even have been exploited and sometimes abused in consequence. And people who have gone astray and who have had terrible things done to them may easily end up doing similar terrible things to others.

People who have done terrible things have commonly in the past (most often in childhood) had similar experiences to those that they have inflicted on others. But why is it natural for human beings to inflict similar pain on others after they have suffered pain themselves? Why do victims become victimisers? Why do we do to others what was done to us instead of treating them as we should prefer to be treated, as Jesus commands (Matthew 7:12)?

This is a clear example of our fallen nature. The fact is that there is a lack of peace in the human soul until there is effective reconciliation with God and the truth of the past as well as the truth of the present is faced. Healing is only built on a firm foundation when Jesus is accepted and received personally as saviour and lord because then the devil has no more rights over you. You may enter God's real presence when you apply the blood of Jesus to your life (Hebrew 10:19). You cry "Jesus shed His blood to save me out of this mess. So Father please heal me!" Patterns of behaviour tend to be destructively repeated until the loving presence and effective authority of God the Father enables the truth to be revealed and forgiveness to be real and demons to go and healing and new life to be received.

Although it is often hard for people who feel bad about themselves to accept His love, the Holy Bible makes it clear that all people can be saved no matter how they are, how they think, or how they feel.

The process of God's healing may take a long time particularly if there is a lot of confusion. But if we persevere under the Lord's direction in His timing what is in the dark comes truthfully and adequately into the light for forgiveness, reconciliation and healing. Putting off the "old man" (Romans 6:6) involves opening the eyes, ears, mind and heart (Isaiah 6:9–10) to how the past unconsciously influences the present. The story must be told (Romans 14:7–12). The heart and mind are changed if the relevant issues from the past are brought into the light of God's truth. Resistance to this difficult business of repentance is overcome as we persevere with Jesus. He heals us and makes us new (2 Corinthians 5:17). But until such matters are sufficiently dealt with there will be a lack of peace and the destructive tendency to continue to repeat old events will remain.

Oedipus

There is another hidden force in fallen human nature, which was known in the mythology of ancient Greece and which was rediscovered by Sigmund Freud. This is the innate tendency to rebel against, destroy and kill the father, without really knowing what we are doing, and naturally to revert to mother-comforts. The Greek story of Oedipus was about a child who was separated from his parents as a baby and who eventually, inadvertently, killed his father and married his mother.

Both the Greek myth and Sigmund Freud were deficient in failing to reveal that it is not only the male offspring who inadvertently rebel against the fathers but also the female. Furthermore, the underlying motivation is far more profound than any hidden sexual desire. It is unconscious rebellion against the essentially priestly nature of the father, made in the image of God, the Father of us all, but inadequate and imperfect due to fallen human nature so that things go wrong and deep disappointments arise and he seems to fail to fulfil his apparent promise of loving everyone unconditionally and keeping everything all right. The natural human being, according to fallen human nature, does not have an intimate relationship with God the Father through Jesus Christ, His Son, and consequently fails truly to know and respect how God created fatherhood in His own image. Nor does the natural human being fully know divine love that truly forgives.

God is far more than we can naturally conceive. Another of His qualities that people naturally find hard to accept is that He has female qualities as well as male. This is particularly revealed in Isaiah 66:13 and Galatians 3:28. He created man and woman in His own image (Genesis 1:27). His masculine assignation includes the feminine in the same sort of way that a wife is given by her father into her husband's family and takes his surname, and in the same way that the soul of both man and woman is assigned the feminine gender[1]. Godly authority in the family is

---

[1] Note for example this verse in a hymn by Isaac Watts (1674–1748): "My soul looks back to see The burden thou didst bear When hanging on the accursed tree, And knows her guilt was there."

exercised in the name of the male, who has a duty of headship (1 Corinthians 11:3). The males, however, will be just as much the bride of Christ as their female partners. But in this world we people have different gifts and men and women are different and God wants us to enjoy the fact. He does not want anyone oppressed by the fact.

One of the universal characteristics of motherhood is unconditional tenderness for the children. I have known mothers who loved and sustained consistently depraved reprobates through thick and thin when the fathers had given up on them long ago. So when fathers fail it is natural to turn to mothers because they can usually be relied upon faithfully to keep essential relationships alive and to keep the home fires burning. It is in this way that a matriarchal society may develop, in which women assume the priestly and protective roles of fatherhood. Women tend to become powerful when men are unrighteous and unfaithful, although women are not generally given the same authority and place as a father and they are more likely to exercise their power in a more diplomatic way, which may naturally become rather manipulative. Fathers complement mothers by exercising spiritual authority and headship (1 Corinthians 11:3).

Men who have disappointed their families, or who have been unfaithful, naturally hide their guilt and shame by ingratiating themselves, often with some degree of pride. In consequence, women will naturally realise that they can manipulate their menfolk. Thus men become venal without realising that their strings are being pulled by their women. The men will look for approbation both to their women and to their male friends, rather than to God, exaggerating their masculinity to try to establish the potency and authority which they have unwittingly lost, and they may easily feel threatened and defensively resentful or violent if that image should be undermined.

Even the best of human fathers cannot make everything all right all the time and they inevitably let us down, which can become the cause of exasperation. Fathers who domin-

ate unjustly or violently are often seen to behave this way to
cover up their own weaknesses. Fathers are rejected so often
because their imperfections, hypocrisy and human failings fail
to earn the real respect of family members. Then, despite good
intentions, the natural, automatic responses of rejection, dis-
appointment and unforgiveness unconsciously lead to destructive responses to fathers. When fathers are rejected there
naturally follows a refusal to know and accept the Godly
authority of fatherhood, and a refusal to honour fathers or to
acknowledge how Father God can heal. In consequence children may become exasperated (Ephesians 6:4) and may turn
towards dangerous paths of rebellion.

The authority of fathers fails to be respected when men do
not recognise God for themselves as their own loving and merciful Father. If they do not turn to their own Father God for
healing their fatherhood is exposed to destructive forces
because they are unrighteous. Fathers do indeed die inadvertently this way.

So a father will naturally tend to fail until he allows himself
to be reconciled to God and allows the Holy Spirit into his
heart. Even then he will fail. But forgiveness and healing can
come if he will bring the Spirit of God into his family. A father's
natural authority will particularly be rebelled against unless he
is seen lovingly to submit, despite his human failings, to the
authority of his Father God in repentance and faith. Then a
good father will be effective in ministering God's words and
ways to his family. When the love and justice of God are apparent in his life, peace will tend to come. Even in the face of dis-
agreement peace will come (Proverbs 16:7).

Rebellion may still cause trouble, however, if there should be
matters that cannot come to light and be acknowledged in the
father's presence. An unwillingness to meet with hm may give
rise to a pressing desire for independence if the shame that
would have to be confessed seems too distressing or too painful
for everyone.

Nevertheless, God wants children and fathers to be reconciled (Malachi 4:6). The relationships that need healing are with both natural fathers and also with other father-figures, including God the Father. When God is allowed to heal relationships with fathers, all the other relationships within families tend towards contentment and we can get free of rebellion sufficiently to live in relative peace. Until that happens there is always resistance against the fatherly gifts with which God imbues men who become fathers and father-figures, and there is consequently some rebellion against God, too, which breeds unrest.

The nature of God may be revealed through a godly man who loves tenderly, who teaches with God's wisdom, who is just and merciful, who provides for his family and guards and protects them[2]. Thus when fathers are reconciled in love to their Father, through Jesus and the Holy Spirit, relationships with those fathers, and within their families, tend to become healed and their families tend to become strong, and they often prosper.

---

[2] The following texts particularly relate to fatherhood: 1 Corinthians 11:3; Ephesians 5:21 – 6:9; Romans 8:12–17; John 8:12 onwards; John 1:12. The first nine chapters of Proverbs ask that Godly wisdom be received by children from their fathers. Malachi asks that the hearts of the fathers be turned to their children and the hearts of the children to their fathers (4:6).

CHAPTER EIGHT

COMMUNITY

Belonging

No matter how much you may sometimes want to get away from other people, it is not possible to be a recluse for long, without negotiation. Isolated day after day, not connecting with other people, you will not be ignored. You will be noticed and folk will talk about you. Unless they can get to know you, and know the sort of thing you are doing and allow you to do it, they will be suspicious of you and will try to discover more about you so that they can know how to respond to you, in order that they may feel safe with you around. You will be aware that they notice you and talk about you and you will begin to wonder what they are saying and thinking. If you start imagining what may be in their minds, without really knowing, you will probably get it wrong and paranoia can creep on fast. There is no alternative but to engage with other people to some extent, in some way or other, and to keep on negotiating your place sufficiently to avoid unwanted trouble.

Of course, if you are perceived as potentially too much trouble but no real threat you may be ignored; although some contact with others will have been necessary at some time in order to have established that opinion of you. This is how old people sometimes come to be forgotten by their neighbours. And this is how people considered to be crazy are tolerated.

So it is human nature to be essentially social. And it is not viable for any one of us to be unilaterally and totally isolated from our own kind for long. Isolation can beget a sense of rejection, which poisons the soul, and a sense of confusion from not knowing where you stand with others.

Although some place or other is usually granted to the lone ranger, the maverick and the traveller, such designations are always taken and held through some sort of negotiation with others. There may have been formal and polite negotiation allowing some hospitality to be offered. Or the negotiation may not have ended in any open agreement and it may have been offensive. An isolated social position may depend only on tacit agreement temporarily not to evict. People may be moved on; but only rarely are they killed for vagabondage or outlawry. Other human beings matter to other human beings, even when the reaction is negative. Those who exclude themselves, or are excluded, from normal society are nevertheless reacting to other people and therefore in some sort of relationship with them.

In this sense we human beings naturally belong together, whether or not we actually manage to do so, and we are naturally driven by social instincts that connect us, even negatively, with other people. There are always natural connections and ties with others and we can only bring our hearts truly to rest when these bonds we have with others are reconciled to God so that all our relationships are right with Him.

Home

The spiritual allegiance with the mother who gave you birth and with the people amongst whom you were reared will always have a profound influence upon you. Your effective family was the first group in which you found a place where you were more or less accepted – enough to survive at least. For the first few years they accepted your smell and cleaned your mess. You had no option but to accept what was offered there, for there was nowhere else to go. If it had not become possible for it to be actually good enough you would probably have died. You took it all in without too much complaint. Those earliest experiences will have formed basic aspects of your personality and character. They will naturally have determined how you think and behave and will always have some influence on your future choices.

Amongst the folk from home, where you come from, there remains some common understanding of what refers to what, and all the implications, and of who defers to whom, and of most of what is inferred when people confer. The common preferences and prejudices are taken for granted. Knowledge of whatever is signified is easily understood. Meaning is held in common. Each of the people who have lived together, sometimes for several generations, brings shared experiences and familiar interpretations of experience to any meeting. Even if the place and community have been destroyed the memories are deeply implanted. You remain familiar with the spirit of the people and the place. The ethos is part of your soul.

In later life you are most likely to feel more settled amongst people who in some way remind you of your old home and seem familiar. If you live fairly closely and share many experiences with them, you may naturally become attached to those people, developing a fondness for them. If you come through hard times together an even stronger comradeship may develop, through having successfully helped each other. You will have built a security together through having proved that you can rely on each other. Military platoons learn to depend on each other in this way, by taking recruits from the same locality and encouraging them through both hard times and good times together. It enables them to look out for each other and protect each other and work together as an efficient unit. Each knows what the other means most of the time, often with minimal explanation.

In order to be included within any group, mutual recognition must develop and familiarity may only come after the breakdown of old prejudices. But unity of spirit is necessary in order to belong. Your own personal spirituality must be acceptable to the others in that group. Essentially, belonging is spiritually determined. Their god must not be offended by your god. Whether or not you really join depends on whether or not you are willing to join in with the spirit of what is going on, the spirit of their god.

The culture of families, firms, groups, communities or nations is predicated upon powerful spiritual influences and presided over by unseen living spiritual beings who influence how things are understood and done (Ephesians 6:12). Events are interpreted and given personal meaning ultimately through spiritual influence. Although the one true God gives sight to everyone (Proverbs 29:13) His way of seeing can be subtly but crucially altered through the influence of other spiritual beings. Communism, humanism, paganism, and so forth, dominate the witting or unwitting worship of the people in particular places. Their influences powerfully determine the nature and patterns of relationship, activity, exclusion and mores (note Exodus 20:4–6, Luke 8:37, etc.).

Moving on

There will frequently be some people unable to join the majority, some people who fall by the wayside, drop out of the community or move away. Sometimes people find they can no longer be at home at home. Some may die. The home may be disrupted, sometimes as a result of war. For some of those people the ethos of the home was inadequate. Others may have needed to explore new pastures. Even with the best intentions in the world, natural groups of people cannot cater for the needs of everyone and in consequence there are always some people who, in one way or another, move on or become excluded. The homes and communities of this world are never perfect. After all, who is truly at home at home?

If you go to live or work in another place, away from the community which has moulded you, you will meet different values, different meanings, different systems of belief and thought; but usually you will be able to adapt because the new culture will not be too strange. The extent to which you join, and consequently the extent to which you are influenced to change, will depend on the extent to which you join in with the spirit of what is going on in the new place.

Then if you return to your old home you will question more of what you once took for granted and will see it more objectively. As George Bernard Shaw once said about his native Ireland, you have to leave it really to appreciate it. Awareness comes from reflection, looking back in the light of new relationships. Although you may still be able to be included in the old community when you go back, you will be more aware of its shortcomings, more critical, more independent, and you are unlikely to take it for granted again. But the folk you used to know will tend to assume you are the same as you used to be and may not recognise how you have changed, which can be frustrating (note Luke 4:24).

Looking back at the inadequacies of the old home can make you long for a better community, one in which the good points are incorporated with more of them, and with none of the faults.

Exclusion

To be on the outside of any personally significant group of other people can naturally produce an unpleasant feeling, even if you are convinced that it was necessary to move away from them. Instinctively we all know there is safety in numbers. There is usually some warmth when people who know each other come together. The desire to belong is natural. A desire to be one of the gang can be powerfully active despite being convinced it is wrong to join. So if it seems to be impossible to belong, a self-protective defensiveness, a resistance to the feeling of being rejected and a self-justification, naturally arises within you. Feeling rejected and vulnerable can lead to insecurity and fear, and in no time at all the sense of reality can become distorted in this way. A person's natural sense of identity is given by other people. Security comes from being known and accepted. Both tend to disintegrate in a person who feels socially excluded.

Proverbs 27:8 says that a person who wanders from home is like a bird who strays from the nest. A person without a home is vulnerable and this can make a person defensive unless a home is found with Jesus (Matthew 8:20).

If the conviction of the need to be separate and stay away from certain people is weak, a person can easily be tempted to compromise in order to avoid being left out in the cold. Despite deep reservations, a person may become willing to collude, willing to suspend judgement and play some sort of social game for the sake of being socially included, and through fear of the consequences of remaining isolated.

Alternatively, a person may go towards new people who seem interesting and get to know them. But they may or may not be people to join with. A person may join to some extent with other folk who have similar interests; but sharing heart and soul so as to be truly at home with them is not so easy. Other folk often are discovered not to have an acceptable spirit. There are many lonely intellectuals.

Increasing numbers of people are becoming socially isolated, never truly at home anywhere. Social contacts are so often ephemeral despite appearances. Many refugees of one sort or another are rootless and economically compromised.

Dislocation is particularly the result of wars and of the break-up of families.

Listening to people who seem different, and trying to understand them so as to relate to their differences and difficulties, is only the beginning of truly including them. It involves not allowing oneself to be prejudiced. It involves loving them. But it need not involve worshipping their gods in any sense at all. Unless the effort is made truly to know them and to be hospitable, they will be unknown and therefore naturally perceived as some sort of threat, and they may consequently be treated oppressively and cruelly and cease to be tolerated. They may form communities of their own within a nation, and worship their different gods, but true community involves common acceptance of acknowledged spiritual authority and its implications.

Institution

The modern word "hospital" derives from the hospitality that used to be offered by Christian monasteries to people who were excluded. They were often wandering, homeless, disturbing, sick, and begging. In the days before the European renaissance of classical Greek thought, and before the subsequent so-called enlightenment, a person could knock on the door of a monastery and if a good enough case were made could often be accommodated for a while in the monastery's hospital. Where groups of Christians lived together there was a tradition of hospitality and care. (Sufficient numbers and sufficient organisation prove necessary in order to care for others.)

Wars and increasing populations undoubtedly increased the numbers of homeless, distressed and distressing people. Many of them probably died of their privations.

When many monastic Christian communal institutions were abolished in Europe, and when communities that had subsisted for generations were broken up, there was insufficient hospitality in society for socially excluded people. Political administrators used empty leper hospitals that were available. Increasing numbers of people who, for one reason or another, had not integrated into society or who were a chronic financial burden on others were socially administered in institutions and prisons. When it became clear that the prisons were not suitable for some of them, it was gradually discovered that much inconvenience could be avoided by the classification of the socially excluded, provided it could be done in a way that was academically acceptable.

Classical thought in Christian cultures changed education and administration sufficiently to assist the increase in prosperity brought about by developing trade and war. As manufacturing industry became concentrated in towns and cities, many people were displaced from their village homes. At the time of the French revolution there was a perceived threat of similar revolution in other nations as many distressed people struggled with poverty and disease. Slavery was abolished about the same time: it became dangerous for any organisation to seem to be too oppressive. Many institutional hospitals were founded and developed around this time. The natural course of different physical illnesses was studied intensively in order to find appropriate ways of managing and treating human distress. Greater efforts were made to differentiate between the idle, the criminal, the poor, the vagabonds, the beggars and the insane. Those deemed unsuitable for prisons were allocated to workhouses and, later still, to asylums.

Further efforts to classify distressing states of mind according to their phenomenology became academically respectable. The consequent means of management and treatment became socially acceptable because they helped human distress to some extent to be put out of sight and out of mind. The concept of psychiatric illness grew greatly in sophistication. Dementia and delirium were distinguished and, later still, schizophrenia. In more recent times selective chemicals have been developed which sufferers can be induced to take in order selectively to modify their perception and behaviour. In this way their trouble and distress can be controlled. Drugs have now become so sophisticated that many psychiatric institutions have been closed because people controlled by these drugs find it possible to live in ordinary society.

The institutional management of the sick was expedient and probably prevented social unrest and revolution. However, institutional relationships tended to be impersonal and regimented. People were pacified by being offered the sort of charity that treats them objectively, by doing something to them or for them to help them. When people are treated like this it is easy for a lack of true compassion to be disguised by the appearance of clinical efficiency. After all, if ever they are truly met and known personally, with the love of God, their distress could be disturbing.

The use of institutions, classifications and drugs has enabled people's distress to be managed so as to be less distressing. The difficulties of truly loving our neighbours as ourselves can be avoided when it is only necessary to concentrate on what has to be done in order to manage (Luke 10:38–42). Impersonal treatment may make it impossible for a person ever to believe that they could truly carry their own load (Galatians 6:5). When the load is classified, labelled, diagnosed and managed by others, a person is being manipulated.

Unless a personal burden is shared (Galatians 6:2) its personal meaning is not being taken seriously by anyone else. So the truth of it can be dismissed. Interpretation can never successfully be imposed on another individual in such a way as to connect a burden with its personal meaning. There is no personal connection with all the implications unless the story is told with meaning from inside the individual heart. When there is no such connection the burden of distress is meaningless. Meaning may be clarified through the responses and suggestions of other people, but it is only the burdened individual who can truly account for the facts. Without connection and meaning there can be no true accountability to God. In consequence it becomes impossible to find the way home to healing.

The word of God teaches us to love our neighbours as ourselves. Neighbours are those who give and accept mercy and hospitality (Luke 10:25–37). Mercy triumphs over judgement (James 2:13). Classical diagnoses are judgements. They may be necessary for management but they can become curses. If we are hospitable and merciful and acknowledge the presence of God who knows the truth of our hearts and loves us nevertheless, we relate personally. Therefore we can assume there is more to a condition than a diagnosis. We can enquire what the place and the meaning of a condition may be in relation to all the other dynamics: "Why has this occurred amidst everything else that is going on?"

Language

There are many people without the opportunity to share what is on their hearts or to explore hidden aspects of their souls. There are many people who have forgotten what it is like to be truly met and heard and known and loved by other people who will keep Godly faith with them. Many people have not found their true voice and many have lost touch with themselves to such an extent that they cannot find what they really need to say. Many, too, have been wounded, and have never been able to open those wounds to healing, so that they are always hiding some part of themselves.

This sort of thing is dangerous because too much lack of personal meaning may cause people to wander away from reality. What they do may lack real meaning. Things may be done to them that are really confusing. If they step outside the social milieu they are used to, they may become lost and bewildered. They can feel most distressingly unreal. There may be nothing left to do but scream; but sometimes that is too embarrassing.

Or instead of a scream, bitterness and boredom may set in with a belief that nothing is real, everything is relative and nothing matters. Many demons are attracted to this sort of attitude. It is a recipe for all sorts of trouble and crime. At least there is hope in a scream (as there is in the yell of a newly born baby). But those who become cynical rebels are buying into death.

Such loss of vital voice comes from not having been sufficiently met, from not having been taken seriously, from having had to put on a face and act the expected part because of some sort of deception, oppression or domination by others, maybe even at "home". Furthermore, a person may have become so used to living a lie that their loss of voice may not be recognised even by themselves. Then they may not realise the extent to which they have become a passive agent of others and have lost their own free will.

If truth should dawn, and the scream begin to come out, who is there to turn to? Who will take you seriously? Who is strong enough to hold you whilst you find your voice? It can be terrifying. It can feel like an explosion waiting to happen that could smash you to pieces. You could lose everything, including the virtual sanity which seems to hold you together.

Or if a person meets Jesus, and the Holy Spirit moves that person into facing truth in deep repentance, with whom is it possible to share it all and make sense of it? For truth to be allowed to dawn so that healing may come, it is surely safest to find other people who are genuinely hospitable and merciful and who have strong enough faith to meet you truthfully without judging you. Sometimes a lot of personal attention will be required over a period of time whilst everything comes to be seen differently (that is, whilst the mind is renewed, as in Romans 12:2).

Many people in these sorts of states may have allowed specialists from institutions to classify them in order that the way they feel and think and behave may be administered and controlled with psychology and drugs. Too often people have used such treatment to give up on the possibility of being truly,

personally met and listened to, and of thereby uncovering their
reality to the Spirit of truth for healing. They have bought the
lie that the treatment in itself is healing. And although they may
really have become hopeless, for fear of rejection they will
usually pretend not to be so.

However, provided a person takes all the institutional language with shrewdness and a pinch of salt, it is in fact possible
to use modern medical treatment sensibly in order to allow
oneself to be held until a time and place is found for God to do
the healing. There is no need to reject institutionalised treatment out of hand. In order to develop sufficient shrewdness to
use it, it is necessary not to believe what other people say until
you can discern the truth of it. You need the discernment which
comes from the Spirit of truth, who is found through Jesus. You
will have to endure being diagnosed, judged to have some
illness, and treated according to some regime or programme.
This need not prevent you from being polite. If ever you should
be asked to comply with a course of action you truly believe to
be wrong, you could politely refuse; there is no point in getting
done in.

It is often necessary for people who wish to be healed
in Jesus' name also to allow non-Christian people to make
diagnoses and give them their treatments. When people are
seriously distressed technological intervention can usually
alleviate their condition. Although there is no need to accept
the judgments of other people (1 Corinthians 2:15) it is necessary to be discerning. When holy scripture speaks about
judging it means coming to a definitive conclusion about what
is going on rather than handing it all over to God for Him to
take care of. Consequently, making diagnoses and using words
which imply that someone has a particular condition that has
an inevitable outcome may in fact be premature judgements
about that person which, if taken to heart, could effectively
curse them. Diagnoses come from the classification of conditions and studies of their natural outcomes. When they are

diagnosed people tend to be put into categories so that they can be managed in institutions and it is relevant that our word "category" comes from the Greek *kategoros* which means "accuser" (see Revelation 12:10). Meanwhile the Christian community can quietly refuse to be held to secular judgements and rather fulfil their duty to other members of the Christian family by continuing to minister with hope for healing in Jesus' name.

The language of classification and administration tends to objectify others and to be abstract. An agent of this sort of milieu may give the appearance of being personally attentive and compassionate but the responses given by you to their conversation and enquiries will be sieved. You may not be met with true authenticity. You may be treated in a calculated fashion. Although that person's mind may be quite willing to accept you in theory, the heart may not be engaged with yours despite appearances to the contrary. The meeting may seem more personal than it is. If you open your heart, you must realise that an alien system of thought may be interposed and the spirit in which any response is given to you may be disguised. If you are particularly needy you can easily be deceived into believing you are truly being met and known. Once this is realised it can easily cause offence. However, there is no need to become bitter, or to start believing that nothing is ever what it seems to be, if you will forgive with Jesus' help. They did not believe Him, either, so He knows.

The mind has the facility of censorship at its disposal to enable it to avoid engagement with the experiences of the body and the feelings of the heart. The mind has the facility to be involved only with an idea and to censor everything personal because to be involved from the heart is always disturbing and often distressing. Those whose business it is to manage illness often cannot afford to have too much heart.

This is the way social games are played. This sort of behaviour enables people involved with administration to get on with the job and not to be too disturbed by all the distress they have to deal with. If they opened their hearts to it all they may need help themselves. People in caring professions are usually fairly well aware of the personal challenges there would be if they were to respond truly personally to the hundreds of people they see who have seriously calloused hearts and prejudiced minds. So they suspend their truly personal feelings and classify according to some academic scheme that gives them worldly authority by having been proved effective for doing the job. Nice though they may be, their job is to hold you rather than to meet you, and rather than to know your heart in truth and walk with you into real healing.

There is so much urgency and trouble and confusion in this world, and so much business to attend to, that there is often little discussion anywhere of feelings and meanings, or of truth and spiritual matters. Sometimes people use political correctness to protect themselves from being offended or disturbed so that they need not become involved in more than they can handle. Sometimes the simple exchange of information passes for real relationship. These ways of talking protect people from gossip or blackmail and from having to bear the frustration of not being met with any true understanding. But such conversation gets boring because it lacks authenticity.

It is far more interesting to speak about what is really on the heart, and about what is really going on in relationships, even when it is disturbing. If you know Jesus the truth can become apparent and it can all be handled by getting right with Him. To be at ease with people you trust, people whose faith is always in Jesus, and to be truly open about what you think and feel, about your relationships and what you have done, enables you naturally to recover, and to gain a more sensible and detached perspective, and to find substantial healing and encouragement.

Sadly, we are all so imperfect that our hearts usually seem to have to be guarded with great shrewdness.

Inclusion

However, some sense of perfect home does seem to live in the imagination of most of us. It may be surmised that it comes from some experience of the womb but I believe it is yet more primitive than that. I reckon it comes from being made in God's image. Somehow we know there is a possibility of home and that one day we could be there for real (Job 19:25–27; Revelation 23:3–4).

Home implies a shelter where we are known and accepted, where we can rest and find healing. It is the place where we deal with our mess truthfully, without having to deny its existence. It is the space in which we can be ourselves amongst people we love, where we are free to open our hearts to be known and loved unconditionally without having to defend ourselves or pretend. It is the place where we are genuinely at ease in loving and being loved, where we truly belong. It is a wholesome sanctuary. God offers us an eternal place like this where we may live with Him; and this may begin to be realised in this world (see Psalm 127:1 and Hebrews 3:6 and 4:9).

Until we begin to come into such a place we shall, to some degree or other, have some sense of having to live with sickness, suffering, stress, anxiety, and alienation. But how may such a place of healing, where we may begin to be at home by being reconciled to God, be found in this world? How may a person come in from the cold so that the love of God may really be known?

We are each naturally programmed to repeat old patterns of behaviour until we find freedom. If healing is not found, the pattern of formative past relationships which have not been healed will be repeated in future relationships. Therefore healing of the past must inevitably be a significant part of any new relationship we want to be at home in.

For example, after a violent marriage a woman went through a traumatic divorce, during which she was said to be unfit to care for her children because of her addiction to alcohol. She had used a lot of liquor for a long time to calm her nerves because of her memories of her father's violence with her. After the divorce she remained so frightened that she could not go out to the shops. Eventually she formed a new friendship with a man who grew to love her but she remained frightened that he, too, would turn violent and find her worthless. She was never able to discuss her previous marriage because she was never able really to tell anyone how she actually had loved her first husband even though he had been so cruel. She was convinced that her new man would be jealous and that the jealousy would turn to violence. She lived with this man for a while but they never married, and eventually they split up and she became very lonely. She became agoraphobic again but another man became sympathetic and found her attractive and so the cycle continued until she was destitute. Even then it continued. Although both booze and men had provided some sort of help and comfort, she nevertheless eventually became homeless because she had never given her account to God in the name of Jesus.

In this sort of situation, healing only comes when it is possible to re-live past experiences, coming to know the meaning of what you are doing and taking responsibility for it in such a way that the old demons are reactivated and become apparent so as to be expelled in the name of Jesus. This lady needed enough people around her to be safe enough to feel at home enough to account intelligently for her fear of violence, her sense of rejection, her habit of rejecting, her loss, and all the rest. She needed safe space for the pain to be admitted and brought into the light, without the fear of other people having traumatic reactions. She needed people she could trust, people the Holy Spirit had brought to maturity. She needed people who had self-control over their natural reactions so that they would not inadvertently collude with her or fall into the trap of having a sexual relationship with her or of abusing her in any other way. She needed space where it was safe for all that was in her heart to become apparent and to be considered in detail before God so that she could receive His love and His authoritative healing.

Where there are people truly in Jesus, the Spirit of love and truth sheds His light and there is freedom (2 Corinthians 3:17). Someone listens and you listen and there is relationship, and Jesus ministers His healing through the relationship. You begin to find true peace as you yield to truth and relinquish patterns of behaviour that trapped you in deadly, repetitive cycles of craving this world's comforts. With truth and peace comes healing. The home you are finding is spiritual.

Such people and such spaces can be found although it is very necessary to be shrewd. No one is perfect in this world but we do discover a foretaste of heaven here and there. Sometimes personal issues are so sensitive that they should only be dealt with very privately by certain mature elders. Sometimes mistakes may be avoided by meeting together with others who have similar stories. Sometimes actually living together in community can be very helpful.

Community

Spiritual unity expressed through the sharing of true meaning that stands the test of challenges (and therefore has authority) is the essence of non-institutional community. Several free individuals come together like the instruments in an orchestra[1] and if the community is truly Christian it is the Holy Spirit who directs all that becomes played out. He gives gifts for the benefit of those who gather (1 Corinthians 12:7) and the authority of Jesus' name may be used in the Spirit for healing.

Dwelling together day by day inevitably causes Christians to apply the gospel in detail in their ordinary personal living. They can do this most effectively if they stop being defensive and speak their truth frankly, submitting to one another, and to God, with love. Community with real relationships is a melting

---

[1] I owe this metaphor to Derek Prince's interpretation of Matthew 18:20.

pot (Proverbs 17:3; 1 Corinthians 3:13 and 4:5) out of which both accurate perception of reality and also self-purification (1 John 1:7) may emerge.

Part of the process of being reconciled to God, and finding healing, is talking openly, albeit with wisdom, with the people with whom you seek to find yourself at home. Through everyday living together you work out where you stand with them with regard to all prevailing issues. The old natural ways of behaving and thinking, which you learned amongst the people with whom you were brought up, need to be recognised and confessed and reconciled to God before healing can occur. When you begin to feel at home, a community can be a substitute family, so old scenarios crop up. If Jesus is present, they can be brought to light by open talk and reconciled to God.

If serious issues from early childhood need to be healed you may need to go right back into childhood in your soul in order to be find healing and change from an early stage of development. In this case you may need to allow yourself to become vulnerable. You may even need the careful, constant protection of eight to twelve other people over a period of months or years. We are not naturally capable of close relationships with more people than this.

Hospitality and accommodation arrangements can take account of the fact that close association of Christian people together in Jesus can be enormously valuable. Sometimes it can enable a person to avoid hospital. The wisdom and guidance of mature elders close to the Lord is essential. But as a splint is to a broken limb so dwelling together in true community with other people in Jesus can hold a person whilst healing takes place by the grace of God.

Other people can hold you whilst you go through what you need to. Sometimes a person may need to be allowed to become distressed or confused or to behave strangely. Provided this is somehow checked out with the others this can be all right. No one should be allowed to lose contact with reality, however.

So it is best for a person to stay in touch with everyday practicalities, although sometimes help may be needed with washing and feeding. For healing to take place, people need to experience unconditionally forgiving but practical love. This can hold them better than drugs or institutions. Freedom of speech is essential because it is through speaking openly that the spirit of the heart is revealed. It is only necessary to respond sensibly according to the Spirit's guidance. We do not actually need to understand everything. It is not for other people to tell a person what issues should be dealt with or what they should be thinking. It is best for a person to use safe space with other Christians to allow the Holy Spirit to bring issues to the surface, and the Spirit should not be quenched (1 Thessalonians 5:19). Eventually the Lord will enable a person to become aware of what needs to be dealt with and He will guide them through repentance and change.

The conversation in truthful communities will often address what is going on fairly directly. Although the entire truth of all that is going on is never absolutely and totally apparent to human beings, the influence of the Holy Spirit reveals aspects of reality that may otherwise be hidden. It will be necessary for everyone to forgive and be forgiven quite often. There is nothing that can be hidden from the Lord (Luke 8:17) and God promises that in the course of time everything will be exposed (Ephesians 5:8–14). But there is a time and a place for everything (Ecclesiastes 3:1–8).

Only where Jesus really is Lord amongst people and the Holy Spirit is at work can there be open and truthful give and take from the heart, and consequent ongoing reconciliation with God, and healing. God requires the Christian community in any place to maintain and defend this sort of interpersonal space (1 Corinthians 3:16–17).

The first Christians found such community together (Acts 2:42–47) and many quickly joined them. But, when they preached their gospel publicly, serious opposition, essentially motivated by envy (Matthew 27:18), came from those who had vested interests in keeping people confined by other beliefs. This served to disperse the first Christians but since the gospel which they took with them could not be suppressed (Matthew 13:33) their message and their kingdom hospitality spread to other places.

Ever since those times there have been scattered Christian communities which have been hospitable places of refuge, good works, healing and evangelism and when they have been powerful in the Holy Spirit they have always faced the same sort of persecution. There have been many martyrs. Some of these communities have been villages, some have been monasteries and some have been looser-knit associations of people living in various places.

Outsiders who do not submit to the spiritual authority of Jesus may not join but, until they accept Him, they may be offered hospitality. Many of those who truly recognise the mess they are in seek spiritual help. The word of God says, "Do to others what you would have them do to you," and "Love your neighbour as yourself." Therefore Christians have an ethical duty to offer healing, and the possibility of real Christian community, within the larger society where they live, and not to hide their light.

No one need be excluded when there is an appeal to the Lord Jesus Christ. All that is necessary in order to be included and to belong is to accept wholeheartedly that Jesus has already paid the price for your sin. God the Father is unconditionally accepting if you truthfully accept a relationship with Jesus and come in repentance just as you are. The love of Jesus will make tolerance and inclusiveness wider and deeper than those of any other sort of community. If one of His disciples suffers all the others suffer with that person too (1 Corinthians 12:26). Such love may seem overwhelming to a newcomer until it is realised that the Lord always enables His people to overcome (Ephesians 1:18–21). "Not by might nor by power, but by my Spirit," says the Lord Almighty (Zechariah 4:6).

CHAPTER NINE

REALITY

What is reality?

I used to know a man called Adrian who had been brought up in a local orphanage and who used to hang around the streets drinking cider. On several occasions, in a mucky, drunken state, he had looked me in the eye and asked me very seriously, "What is reality?" And I knew he was in such a rough way because he was unable to answer that question himself.

In John 18:38 we are told that Pilate asked a similar question at Jesus' trial: "What is truth?"

I took Adrian's question about the nature of reality very seriously. I knew he was genuinely troubled by it. And since I had never managed to come out with a rejoinder that seemed to satisfy him, I asked my wife, Pamela, the same question that he had asked me. Quick as a flash she said, "Oh! Reality is the experience of truth."

Thus I was enabled to see that, through the experience of the senses, reality may be perceived by receiving truth, which is spiritual (John 3:21). Now, that is profound and that is the hub of it. But this is an issue which troubles many people, particularly those who have come to doubt the sense they once made of their experience.

Many people do not know how to find truth. And if they do begin to perceive truthfully they may not know how to face it. The problem is often whether or not what is being perceived is true, whether or not actual reality is being perceived, whether or not perception is free of distortions, denials and deceptions, and how to handle meaning when it becomes apparent.

We are prone to illusion. We cannot be sure of the truth and we easily become sceptical about what we seem to see and hear and perceive and understand, and about what other people tell us. Although we may know how we feel, and know it to be authentic, the full truth of why we feel as we do, and of the nature of what we are considering, may be hidden from us. Classically, perception through the senses is acknowledged to be liable to distortion and it is traditional to doubt it. It is considered to be in need of proof. The evidence of our senses needs to be shown to be incontrovertibly valid and consequently we nowadays believe that truth can best be discovered through scientific experiment and measurement. Because we doubt, we trust only what we human beings can measure.

The question arises, however, whether or not scientific experiment and measurement can take adequate account of other spiritual influences (scientific measurement itself being under the spiritual influence of scepticism – see Exodus 30:12, 2 Samuel 24:10 and 1 Chronicles 21) because if you change your spiritual allegiance you see things differently. The same measurements mean different things to different people. Strict sceptics will say that spiritual influences are not real. But there seems little doubt that people with different beliefs make different value judgements and that trusting only human reason is just one of many possible spiritual paths. The interpretation and use of scientific evidence, and therefore its meaning and reality, differ according to the influence of allegiances that are relational and spiritual. And when people change in these respects the circumstances are seen to change. Different aspects of truth appear as relationships change. We see things in the light of the personality of our god and in the light of what is acceptable in the culture in which we belong. Our sense of values, our knowledge of good and of evil, comes from the god whose truth we accept. For Satan, what a Christian calls evil may be good, and so on.

When we accept that Jesus died on the cross to redeem us from our sins and rose from the dead the third day, and when we make Him our lord and saviour and decide to follow Him, the Holy Spirit ministers the truth of God to us and gives us discernment and guidance in the use of what we perceive, and in giving it meaning.

The people on whom you have depended may sometimes have said one thing but meant another and only much later may you have come to begin to realise the truth of what perhaps they may really have meant, and what may really have been going on. Moreover, true aspects of reality, different from what had hitherto been assumed, may sometimes become apparent quite suddenly. Then, as new meaning dawns, the new awareness may sometimes appear so painful that you put it out of your mind. It may even threaten to undermine the very foundation of much that you had hitherto taken for granted. From that moment forward, for a while, your sense of security is likely to be shaken. But how may you really know if your doubts really have any foundation in truth?

A woman asked how her father could have loved her as he had said he did, and as she had hitherto believed he did, when he had been having sexual intercourse with her from a very early age. She had eventually come to realise that this had not permitted her to be free. The realisation that it could be possible to have her freedom, if she could face the true facts and find healing, was devastating. She spent many years in psychiatric units and she lost hope because it all seemed too much for her.

A young man suddenly realised that he had loved his family, and that they had loved him, but that he had felt overwhelmingly rejected when they had been unable to accept his hatred of them following a sudden move of house away from his friends when he was a young boy. His hatred and resentment had caused him to rebel and to be aggressive for many years. But then he had a perforated duodenal ulcer and nearly died. By a miracle he met Jesus after having been visited in hospital by a Christian friend and as a result he came to a place where he could accept forgiveness for the hurt he had caused to so many people. Then, in his brokenness and repentance, he realised he needed to forgive his parents. When he did so it was remarkably healing for all concerned. He is now peaceful and well and a thoroughly changed man.

A marriage deteriorated to the point of divorce: He saw things one way. She told a very different story. The marriage guidance counsellor could make no accurate assessment of the truth of what had gone on therefore it seemed necessary to make no judgements about it.

A couple retired at the age of fifty-five with a pension sufficient for comfort. They spent their time travelling and making their home nice. They involved themselves in charitable work and were active in their local church. When they got ill the doctor was a friend and their private health insurance enabled the trouble to be fixed as expeditiously as possible. They claimed to be unable to understand why people should become addicted to drugs and why there were so many dysfunctional families in the estate on the other side of town. They said their experience of life gave them no insight into why people should become so distressing.

Another man had never discussed anything very much with anyone ever in his life – never with the sort of discussion that requires consideration of how other people may have felt and thought about things. And no one had ever seemed bothered about how he thought or felt about anything, either. School had been boring. It had always been possible to avoid any misery by doing something to take his mind off it, even if it was only watching a programme on television. Nothing seemed to have much meaning for him. Work served the purpose of getting food and a house. His partner seemed to enjoy the same sort of entertainment as he did and both of them liked to spend hours on computer games. Then suddenly he had an accident in his car in which someone was killed. He ran away from the scene. Eventually he was arrested and imprisoned. His partner found someone else to live with and took their children and possessions. A girl who had happened to visit another prisoner was soon the only person to visit him regularly in prison. For some people nothing ever means anything of much significance. Or does it? When there was a riot in the prison this man was one of the ringleaders and he became so violent that he killed another man. Now he is serving life.

In the humanities departments of universities it has become fashionable to read texts in various ways so that meanings may be exposed which differ from the meanings which hitherto had been assumed. Cultural and conceptual bias may, it is supposed, be eliminated by reading texts in different ways so that it becomes possible to open up all sorts of new interpretations. Although this may originally have been done in an attempt to discover ground wherein the soul may be firmly anchored, in the hope of being free to give authentic expression to genuine meaning and in order perhaps to discover truth, the process of deconstruction has commonly become a fashionable end in itself.

An intelligent child may take a machine to pieces in order to discover how it works but, without the father's guidance, may be unable to put it together again so that it works. When the father's guidance cannot be received – because of the child's rebellion or sometimes because of the father's rebellion – the child may cynically continue this sort of deconstructive activity and eventually, through habit, destroy much of what the father had known and built without being able to replace what was destroyed with anything of any lasting worth.

Although modern solutions may seem to be efficient, they are often just patching up this sort of rebellious destruction, which goes on all the time. It may be seen as a manifestation of the unresolved Oedipus complex, that is, of the innate tendency of fallen human nature to turn away from Father God and kill-off fathers. For those who become locked into this cynicism, reality is hopeless, there is no wisdom worth believing in and any suffering often seems pointless. Modern technologies may be used to satisfy every passing need and fancy and to avoid pain as much as possible. No truth of any absolute worth is recognized. Sadly, this is an increasingly common view of reality.

As these examples demonstrate, everyone may have their own personal truth which extends as far as they can see. But there is no recognition in any but the second of the examples that what is seen is just a facet of a much greater reality and that the absolute and eternal truth of God may, in fact, help human beings (Psalm 121:1–2).

This is not to say that any human being could ever claim to have a monopoly of God's truth (see 1 Corinthians 13:9 and Philippians 3:12). It is simply to profess that God's interest in our lives causes His truth to be revealed to us, and that perceiving it is part of His healing.

God reveals His truth to people when they humble themselves before Him and ask for His help and healing and salvation (Deuteronomy 30, 2 Chronicles 7:14). Consequently, to some extent or other we have to suffer, to "allow" (as in Matthew 19:14), and to let go of our pride and rebellion and pain[1] in such a way as to be open enough to receive His truth. In this sense, pain is the opposite of suffering. Pain is resistance but suffering is opening up to Jesus in the agony rather than

---

[1] Letting go of our pain may expose our woundedness so that we suffer the hurt and vulnerability. Pain is much more severe when we resist it and try all we can not to feel it. We should yield it to Jesus (Isaiah 53:5, 1 Peter 2:24, 4:19, 5:7).

fighting it all off to make it go away. We suffer when we let Him take it and allow Him to see us through and let Him open our eyes and ears and soften our hearts.

There is no point in being disappointed that God reveals His truth in suffering, because He is in charge and He loves us and knows what has happened and all that is going on (see Hebrews 2). When we ask God for help in the name of Jesus and ask Him to save us and to show us what to do, He sends His Holy Spirit to lead us into repentance so we may be reconciled to God through forgiveness and healing. His Holy Spirit also gives us the discernment and courage to leave false cultural values and be real. When we accept Jesus, God's truth begins to become apparent to us. The Holy Spirit will show us a way through whatever we have to go through, and show us a way out to freedom. And He will continue to help us to be rid of everything that gets in the way of healing.

Although we may even have to confess the sinfulness of our natural reactions to extreme abuse and provocation, God will bless our truthfulness with His healing and comfort when we stop trying to justify ourselves. Jesus is the truth, the way and the life (John 14). He can be our only justification. This makes us thankful in spite of ourselves.

The vision of Christians and non Christians alike may be limited, blinkered, restricted. But people who do not know Jesus live in a more partial reality. They may tell it how it is according to them but it will only be one facet of the account to be given. If they do not know how to approach God, through accepting Jesus, to find the wisdom to face the partial truth they see, their reality will be composed of inventions which ultimately fail to satisfy.

After two world wars, and whilst such terrible destruction continues in so many places, it may sometimes seem to many people as though God has abdicated or, as Hegel said, "God is dead". In the same vein, it may seem hopeless when a father deserts a family so that the woman and children have to fend for themselves, or when those who are in charge seem to fail to keep things all right. It may seem as though there is no way out of the hell you are living in.

But God is not dead. The power that raised Jesus from the dead is very much alive. In the shock and trauma of the worst wars and devastations we may turn to Him and receive His direction and know His presence (Deuteronomy 31:6; Matthew 28:20). In fact such devastations were prophesied in Scripture. It is necessary to bear in mind that evil has a right to enter into situations where the people do not acknowledge and worship God in Spirit and in truth, when they turn away from Him and cease to heed Him.

Those who return to Him in repentance, accepting the Lord Jesus Christ of Nazareth, and who then listen carefully to His voice, will be saved by Him (Leviticus 26, Deuteronomy 28, 1 Timothy 4:10) through whatever they have to go through. In their suffering they will be comforted by Him. They will be shown enough of their reality to find sanity. He will provide for them (Isaiah 30:20–21).

Security

It is human nature to build on what has seemed to make sense previously. By nature we form particularly strong attachments to the people and concepts and things which have seen us through the vicissitudes of the past. Members of our close family, the people with whom we have formed a strong bond tempered by adversity, and the beliefs and things associated with them, all signify allegiance to a culture that has hitherto made sufficient sense for us.

Only if our hearts and minds are unusually opened are we likely to question what we have always taken for granted. However, times suddenly come to many of us that shake us up so badly that we no longer seem to know what to do. With natural disasters, serious loss, rejection, war, death, disease, oppression, and so on, everything in which we once put our faith is challenged. Furthermore, new technologies and changing culture open up new possibilities which make urgent demands. When serious devastation comes into our lives, or when everything is shaken up, the wisdom and beliefs of the past may suddenly seem inadequate. Past experience then seems to fail to provide adequate resources for strange circumstances. We become tempted in ways we never dreamt possible.

In a desperate attempt to win through and to avoid losing face, or to avoid falling to pieces, quick decisions have to be made. We may come to conclusions and take decisions which appear to provide sufficient natural ground and semblance of reality in order to recuperate. Later, however, they may seem to have been premature. Some people may hold out, and maintain entrenched positions holding onto old ways But generally there will seem to be no time or inclination seriously to seek God for His direction or to consider afresh God's lessons from history. As the ways and beliefs of our forebears are inevitably questioned, age-old wisdom from God gets jettisoned for fear of seeming irrelevant as fashion changes – and for fear of being alone in realising its relevance.

We naturally invent new things and ideas, and develop relationships and interpretations of reality which seem expedient, and they rapidly become our new security. As the new takes over from the old it soon seems that if we were to let go of our new ways there could again be some risk of everything falling apart. We usually fail to concern ourselves with the actual nature or name of the spirit by which such modernisation is being led.

We hold on to acceptable routines, and social customs, and to what people say, and to fashion. We hold on to our possessions and money for our security, and to our jobs. We hold on at all costs to the ways of seeing and doing things which seem practical, and to the objects which have been significant for us. We hold on to what we are told in the media, and to what leaders and charismatic figures tell us. But we avoid looking at less obvious issues, particularly if they seem uncomfortable or painful. So we fail to take into account the mind of God.

We hold on tenaciously to what seems to make immediate sense because it feels good, in the same way that an addicted person is unable to let go of the craving for a substance. It is human nature to hold on obsessively to what we have made up our minds to be the case, and thus to be locked into a culture. Changing the mind, so as to have thoughts that are different from the majority of other people, is risky. Would you risk losing your friends or even your job and your mortgage for what is right with God?

Under threat of loss of money, security, prestige, a surprising number of people would do anything to keep their jobs, even despite employers' subtle demands that they effectively undermine their morality by compromising what they believe to be right and true.

Whom do you respect enough to allow to influence you towards the sort of change that could be costly? It is easier to stick with the facts as you see them and turn a blind eye to the strongholds of prejudice which have formed in consequence of your limited vision.

Unreality

It is natural to shut out of the mind whatever causes too much pain or anxiety and whatever is too much to understand immediately. Our automatic censor causes us to forget and to be unaware of whatever we do not seem to have the resources to cope with. We do not see more than we seem to need to see. The aspects of our own past experience which are unhealed, and things we cannot make sense of, are censored and cut out of awareness. We need to get by in life with the minimum of trouble. "What the eye does not see the heart does not grieve over," says the old proverb. This way we hope to be able to cope.

But what the eye does not see and the heart does not grieve over may suddenly become apparent to us. And when that happens it is a God-sent opportunity to change the mind (James 4:9–10). Until the heart is impacted with an imperative the censor prevents the person seeing more than is necessary to maintain the old strongholds of prejudice and an expedient sense of security.

Demonic powers, sometimes of a high order, use the strongholds of our prejudices, and our confusion or fear, in order to try to control us. Demonic powers attach themselves to the deceptive ways in which we have made up our minds. If people give them any legal right to do so demonic powers will manipulate and dominate human beings in order to deceive us into courses of action which are ultimately destructive. They gain the legal right to take hold of a person's life when someone effectively calls on them to reinforce a stronghold, often with a curse, whether or not those people know what they are doing.

If different spiritual paths are then followed under demonic influence, different realities begin to appear. For example, I have known one or two people who were quite convinced that they had been abducted by aliens. Demons are implacably opposed to the eternal kingdom of God. They operate in astonishingly deceptive ways. They know very well who Jesus is, even if we do not, and they oppose Him to the utmost of their power. They attempt to control not only individual people but also whole groups, societies and nations.

Sadly there are many people who live in cultures far removed from what the Christian knows to be real. Even in societies which were Christian until recently, meanings have crept in which are ephemeral, and devoid of sufficient truth to afford lasting satisfaction. Apparent solutions are brought to bad situations with remedies that are modern but which, on deeper investigation, are often found to lack Godly wisdom and righteousness. Cultures are manipulated away from true reality by the clever use of psychology in order both to control media presentation and to sell through advertising.

If there is no thought of being accountable to God, the only available security is to try to be who you should be according to the manipulative information you receive about how to behave in the culture you aspire to, regardless of any real, true meaning (which you have ceased to believe exists anyway). To a surprisingly large extent these days a person's reality and apparent security can be composed of advertised brand images and signs, each of which signifies a constellation of feel-good factors and connected data. Images that are believed in are idols and God is provoked to anger by false worship (e.g. 1 Kings 14:9). When sudden changes happen this sort of reality is easy to destabilise.

However, the reasoning of governments has to be protected against excessively destructive criticism that could cause revolution. And goods need to be sold for profit to maintain the economy. Therefore psychological science is used with cunning to manipulate opinion. This is the human answer to the difficulty of governing in alarming times in an information-saturated democracy. It has supplanted Christian wisdom and prophetic guidance in an age in which the older Christian denominations have lost much of their respect and their faith following the challenging devastations of two world wars.

A virtual reality has been created out of the need to pacify people whose simple faith has been shattered. The basis of the old application of Christian values to every area of life has been radically questioned since the two world wars and substitutes have been created out of human reason and expediency. The need to pacify every other religion has led political leaders to support syncretistic multifaith solutions for a multicultural society in which real meaning is up for grabs.

The realisation that ephemeral and manipulated solutions are inadequate will probably only become apparent when they cease to maintain adequate peace. Christians and Jews with sincere faith in the God of peace will probably be increasingly persecuted. Truth is often too much to face without Jesus. The only begotten Son of God is the only one to have overcome the world but there is terrible resistance to opening the eyes to this fact. It is impossible to return to the sound realities of Christian society without repentance; but repentance may involve suffering and it is necessary for there to be repentance in the church. Perhaps there will be sufficient people of faith left to help to minister God's healing to those who turn back to Him in repentance and who cry out to Him for help amidst the lawlessness.

If the circumstances of people's lives change drastically, however, their confusion and unawareness of truth may be so profound that it may seem almost impossible for them to find access to how to make sense. The extent of the truth of which a person is not aware is sometimes enormous. Sometimes a person may actually feel unreal, and say so. In this case it is necessary to go back to where contact with reality was lost. For healing to occur the story must be told and the truth must dawn into it. If a person is full of shock, fear, grief, unforgiveness, hatred, or hopelessness their perception will be affected.

A person may have become so used to that sort of situation that it may seem quite normal. There are many people whose contact with reality is more tenuous than it seems to be, although most are unaware of the fact.

Brokenness

A soldier had been very distressed at having to clear up body parts of children after terrorist explosions on active service. He managed to cope by putting the thoughts and memory of those experiences out of his mind and by cultivating attitudes of hatred towards ethnic groups similar to those who had committed the atrocities. His demons of hatred and violence, which he had inadvertently cultivated, actually helped his military career. They made him seem hard and fearless. But they wrecked his family because those who knew him intimately became distressed by his intolerance and lack of compassion and his constant need to be physically active in order to avoid boredom. To them he had changed after his exceedingly distressing experiences on active service; he, however, denied it. His hatred and anger would suddenly flare up and distress them deeply but, he always justified himself.

When his wife eventually left him he became very tearful and quite scared for an extended period of time. Whenever he left work he would become very sad and for a long time he was frequently tempted to commit suicide although he was able to hide the fact and put on a good face for other people. He began to realise how cruel he had sometimes been to his wife. One day he went with a friend to a Christian church and it dawned upon him when he said the Lord's Prayer that if he was going to be forgiven he, too, had to be willing to forgive. One day he realised that even though he did not feel like it he had to forgive those terrorists who had caused such heinous outrage – for his own sake, if for no one else, in order to find peace for his mind and soul. Some people from the church, to whom he mentioned this, prayed for him in the name of Jesus and he eventually became willing to do so. God does not despise a broken and a contrite heart (Psalm 51:17) and He responds with His comfort to those who accept Jesus. He faced all the shock and all the trauma that he had been putting out of his mind for so long. It was profoundly disturbing but he was eventually healed and set free from demons of hatred and fear and violence through Christian prayer. He discovered that forgiveness frees the heart and that when Jesus lives in the heart it becomes clean. His opinions, his whole outlook and his behaviour changed. He could show love much more spontaneously and was loved much more openly by his children. He began to win the trust of his military superiors for his foresight and stability under pressure, and he was promoted.

Sometimes God allows us to be very seriously shaken so that we let go of our old ways of seeing and take hold of His truth. But to be faced with a need to consider concepts about yourself to which you have never previously been introduced can provoke a lot of anxiety. It is natural to resist thoughts about yourself which are out of the ordinary and which may make you vulnerable. It was natural for this soldier to resist thoughts of forgiveness and of being less aggressive. Such thoughts threatened his livelihood. But the Holy Spirit ministers God's truth gently, with love. He drives out fear (1 John 4:18) and then it becomes safe to change the mind as His truth becomes credible through the outworking of real relationships.

Although we do not usually allow ourselves to acknowledge the fact, the thoughts and attitudes on which we have built our reality frequently lack firm foundation in the truth of God. Nevertheless, they may still serve to protect us from unmasterable anxiety, dread and fear. These shaky securities, which we cling on to, are adequate until their deficiencies become apparent. Often, the first sign of their inadequacy is boredom. But in their lack of faith people often say, "better the devil you know than the devil you don't" and consequently they stick with what they know rather than explore new territory.

Letting go of what, in the past, has seemed to make sense and provide firm ground for being assertive, naturally causes anxiety. And we would naturally do anything to avoid having to face it. Sometimes a person may even develop a feeling that to let go of the way the mind has been made up could cause the loss of all reason, and cause actual madness. If every point of reference should be lost, what would be real? Would truth appear?

Techniques of brainwashing have sometimes been used by totalitarian regimes to demolish what they consider to be undesirable cultural influences in prisoners. Conceptual securities and systems of belief which have hitherto composed the mind are systematically undermined. Even old habits are broken so that eventually there is nothing left to hold on to. The intention is to impose new ways of thinking and behaving which alleviate the anxiety and dread. In this way, dedication to systems of belief which had previously seemed totally alien can successfully be induced. Acceptable answers to desperate needs and questions can be provided by dogma, domination, manipulation and control and a new set of values can be accepted. To someone living in the freedom of a strong personal relationship with Jesus this will appear to be oppressive but to someone who does not know Jesus it can become the reason for living.

The sense of reality may, however, be lost without this pressure to adopt a new set of values and beliefs. Changes of circumstance may be so confusing, and natural reactions to oppressions and difficulties may become so overwhelming, that a person may be said to lose their mind.

Confusion, insecurity, strong emotions and altered perception may lead to behaviour which other people find strange. I remember a professional woman who was in such a state that all that seemed to make sense to her was what she excreted. She sat and played with her faeces and was confused by anything else.

In this sort of lostness, only unconditional love – loving your neighbour as yourself – proves worthy of faith. Such love comes to us from God through Jesus and it is found in people who know the love of God either personally through Jesus or through the family in which they were reared. There is always personal freedom in it, never judgement or oppression. Words of love are not enough: they are only credible if they are accompanied by authentic deeds (James 2:14–26). If you find kind people who are patient and who do not hurt you, and who speak truth and make sense and keep faith with you, fondness and love grow reciprocally and salvation may be found.

The process of repentance and changing and renewing the mind is a process of letting go of strongholds of prejudice and getting rid of demons and accepting the revelation of truth through the Holy Spirit. There is often a natural anxiety and vulnerability. Staying safe involves accepting some sort of hospitality from kind people who can meet you faithfully in love and truth, without taking any advantage of you, at the time when you may have little to hold on to.

This sort of practical hospitality, with patience, is necessary to enable broken people to repent and renew their minds and build their lives in Jesus. This sort of space cannot be sustained without supernatural resources. And in order to have that protection it is necessary to worship the God who provides it and to act openly in His name. People need other people who know Jesus in order to help them make sense and find their way without being deceived. This is the proper Christian alternative to secular treatments (James 1:27, 5:19–20; Romans 12:13; 1 Peter 4:9–11).

The truth will set you free

One of the stumbling blocks in repentance these days is the time it often takes for habitual reactions of the soul and body to adjust to the new life in Christ. You can be distressed or sad when you begin to realise the truth of what you have hitherto been involved with. Then, when you do not feel the way you think you should feel, you may seek a convenient way of changing how you feel without giving God enough time to take you through all the issues and heal you thoroughly. You may go to the doctor for something to make you feel better. Few doctors, Christian or not, have a true understanding of the spiritual dimension and most are likely to make a scientific diagnosis which will result in scientific treatment. The scientific treatment may reinforce the conviction that you should not be feeling as you do and the diagnosis may reinforce the conviction that you are ill. So if you are not careful you are liable to believe that facing the actual truth in repentance is dangerous or impossible because when you get into what you thought was repentance you end up being called ill.

To get out of this mess you must see the situation in truth and to do this you need the Holy Spirit in you. The danger is that unless you feel the pain and sadness, and all the other feelings necessary to put you in touch with true reality, you may be so out of touch with your body that repentance will not be real. Emotions are necessary in order to begin to know the truth of what is going on. Emotions put you in touch with reality but for freedom they must be submitted to the Spirit of God living in you. God provides freedom through Jesus who died to save you. If your emotions are liable to get out of hand, find other people you trust with God's love and truth in them and tell them what you feel and allow them to hold you and contain you so the Lord can heal you. In emergency there is always the doctor – or the police. But usually it is necessary to suffer strong emotions for a considerable time so that your body and soul may work through all the issues connected with them as the Lord heals you.

What is commonly called depression may sometimes be caused by the oppressiveness of the dilemma of who to turn to and what to believe. When by the grace of God the true reality of the situation begins to dawn, it can sometimes seem overwhelming. Sometimes the accurate perception of reality can be very distressing (John 1:5, 10, Jeremiah 20:7–18) and cause strange reactions until God's peace comes. However the situation can sometimes be made much worse by assuming that you are irrevocably ill. If you are unable for a time to find anyone who understands it may be reasonable to find some medicine to hold you and for this you will need a doctor. Let the doctor think in medical terms but you hold to what God is saying.

There is nothing essentially wrong with using medical and psychological treatment. It can sometimes be expedient to be held for a while by drugs or in a professional relationship, or both. It may be right to use these. But Jesus says, ". . . the truth will set you free" (John 8:31).

So it is all right to be sad, and to have a whole host of other profound emotions, if you are in contact with God and His truth and His word through the Holy Spirit and if His people are around you and your relationships with them are good enough. Reality is not just all the bad stuff, it is God as well – who heals if we love and follow Jesus. He releases our emotions and reveals the truth of our human nature, and of our predicaments, and of our sin, and He takes it all and shows us the way though it and eventually out of it. The process takes time, sometimes a long time. If we endure and persevere God develops His character and real hope in us (Romans 5:3–4, James 1:12, 2 Timothy 2:12). God allows you to have unpleasant emotions in order that you may experience truth in this world and know his salvation.

There is no reality without suffering, or indeed without some degree of anxiety, lostness and madness. Reality is only perceived when there is true healing for suffering. And we may have to lose our way in order to find it. But when we are lost it is essential to be most careful whom we call on. Whichever god we invoke will come to guide us. It is only the God of Abraham, Isaac and Jacob, whom Jesus called "Father", who leads the way to abundant life with Himself beyond time (Revelation 10:6, KJV). He promises that if we ask we find Him. We need to ask clearly using the name of Jesus Christ of Nazareth His only begotten Son and accepting that this Jesus died for our sin and rose from the dead the third day. Then we hear His words through receiving His Holy Spirit.

If you insist on being positive all the time, and in always looking on the bright side, you will be living in denial of often-painful reality. For Jesus reality was the cross. When our human nature conflicts with God's will and revelation, to stay real we must take up our cross and suffer with Him.

God allows us to come down to earth in order to work out our salvation for real and change to become more like Him. We change through allowing Him to adjust and change what we block out from our awareness and by being delivered of every wrong spirit. His light makes everything visible (Ephesians

5:14). He provides us with the ability to see what has been hidden in its true light and consequently to put it in its rightful place.

The parts of our physical bodies that are usually hidden and forgotten are not to be denied but are to be seen in a way that is right with God (1 Corinthians 12:21–26). Work this world does not consider respectable and people not reckoned successful by the standards of this world are not to be considered insignificant but are to be seen in a way that is right with God (James 1:9–11 and 2:1–9). And the experiences, thoughts and feelings that this world tries to hide by controlling them, through medical science and other camouflage, are not to be denied but are to be seen instead in the light of truth and given their true meaning (Ephesians 5:8–15).

God gives us essential practical work, like getting food and fixing our clothes and shelter, and He gives us everyday routines, like having to wash and excrete, in order to keep us down to earth and to keep us in touch with reality and remind us not to live in a fool's paradise. When we suffer it is as well to keep in touch with these necessities so as not to allow spirits of self pity and infirmity to control us, although it is also necessary to be humble enough to accept help from others. Furthermore, we are all conceived and born amidst our mother's intimate body fluids, and we all die so that our bodies have to be disposed of by others, and we cannot control the facts of these events. God gives us opportunities to face simple realities of our existence so that we should not become disconnected from what is truly credible.

He also allows us hurtful experiences and burdensome emotions. Sometimes we need the rebukes of other people (Luke 17:3). Sometimes we need to face the consequences of our mistakes. Sometimes we need to face the consequences of other people's mistakes. Sometimes we need to see and feel the terrible mess we are in and our world is in. All this God will use for His own purposes to sort us out both individually and collectively in a way that is right with Him (James 1:2–7) so that we may find healing and holiness.

So it is necessary always to question whether or not the way we perceive what is going on is accurate, and to allow Him to reveal truth into our experience. It is necessary to ask the Holy Spirit to reveal whatever we may be avoiding and to check us if we perceive in a wrong spirit (1 John 4:1). It is also necessary to be aware that often, when God's redeeming hand is at work, people who do not know Him mock, because all they can see is the fate and gloom this world habitually associates with suffering. Christians are not subject to human judgement (1 Corinthians 2:14–16). Persisting and enduring through all this sort of thing is the way disciples of Jesus put off the old self and become a new creation, as described in 2 Corinthians 5:17 and Ephesians 4:22, etc.

Sometimes we may have to go back in order to make sense of the past and grow up again with healing – usually not only in our mind and memory but also in our actual behaviour. To find God's healing for the past we may have to allow ourselves to go back into it. Sometimes we may have to be quite childish for God to heal what went wrong. We may have to regress to some extent and go backwards in order to come forwards again. We may even need surrogate parents for a while, and other people who are like family. When this happens it does not last for ever. Unless we get into what we need to get out of, we may stay lost. In every stronghold the way in is the way out. To some extent you have to make a fool of yourself to find healing. While this is going on it helps a lot to stay in touch with the simple practicalities of life such as eating and washing, and so on.

We first grew up with the help of our parents but they will eventually grow old, and they may have died. By the grace of God, we eventually discover that we can manage without them. In order to grow to maturity we need to have built true meaning into our souls and bodies through relationships with the people and things of this world. But there comes a time when we have to let go of each of the people and things that helped us. Although we may mourn for what has gone, our grief is only the natural response of the soul. God will build on the truth of the past to move us into new territory if we allow ourselves to be guided by His Holy Spirit and allow Him to reveal to us the course we should take. So it is incumbent upon the church to be hospitable and messy, as folk heal and grow in the Lord. This is how He leads us into His truth. And the closer we grow to Him the more reality is apparent, and the more we worship.

CHAPTER TEN

ILLNESS

Spiritual origin

It is never God's desire that anyone should be ill. The God of Abraham, Isaac and Jacob, whom Jesus called Father, is the God who heals (Exodus 15:26). When Jesus healed people He was doing what His Father was doing (John 5:19). God's nature is to heal to the uttermost (Acts 3:16; 1 Corinthians 1:4–9; 1 Thessalonians 5:23–24). Those who come into His presence may expect healing.

Illness comes upon us, however, through our collective failure to maintain a good and right relationship with God from generation to generation. This is described clearly in Leviticus Chapter 26 and Deuteronomy Chapter 28. God is just and pure and faithful. In order for there to be healing, it is necessary for people to have a personal relationship with Him in love and to worship so that their hearts are open to Him without hindrance. In this fallen world we have to do battle with all that gets in the way of our relationship with Him and we can only wage effective war against it all if we invite the Holy Spirit to live in us with His power. Although He never takes His love away, He cannot bestow the blessing of health and healing on people who turn away from Him, whether they do it knowingly or unknowingly (Isaiah 6:10).

Since we have been created by nature to be social, to be in relationships all the time with other people, both spiritual and physical, it behoves us to keep all our relationships right according to our creator and to maintain a right relationship with Him (1 John 3:21). We are all in this world together and are created to be our neighbours' keepers to some extent (Genesis 4:9, Psalm 35:13–14, Luke 10:25–37, etc.) and consequently the sin of both the company we keep and also the society we live in wears off on us, whether we like it or not. Therefore even the most Godly people get ill. Illness is endemic in a sick and fallen world.

Furthermore, the natural reactions of our fallen nature take their toll on our bodies. Every aspect of every relationship produces exquisite changes in the physiology of the body. And each one of us inherits both physical and personality characteristics from our ancestors and from their imperfections (Exodus 20:5, Deuteronomy 23:2–3). Therefore it may be said that three groups of spiritual factors contribute to the presence of illness in our lives, namely the sin of the society in which we live, our personal fallen human nature, and the inherited sin of our ancestors. Nevertheless, there should be no doubt that there are times when God overcomes all this in an instant and heals with power in order that His nature should be revealed in this world (Luke 5:17–26).

Like the blind man whose healing is reported in John 9, the illness of some of those people who do not have a right and lively personal relationship with God may nevertheless be nothing to do with the sin of their ancestors or with their personal sin. However, the healing of the paralysed man reported in Luke 5 connects his illness with his sin very clearly.

It is commonly assumed that pure chance determines who is afflicted when, and how, with illness. Some scientists, and even some philosophers, may assume that all illness can be explained scientifically, although final causes are rarely, if ever, addressed by them. The physical aetiology and pathogenesis of every sort of illness have been subjected to meticulous scientific research, but the spiritual and relational aspects have scarcely been considered because they have been deemed contingent upon belief and therefore irrelevant to science.

However, those with godly discernment and courage may perhaps permit themselves to see that illness strikes at the weak points, which are not only the weaker individuals in society but also the points of conflict in the individual body, soul and spirit where what a person wants, thinks, or feels conflicts with what is right with God.

For example, some time ago it was becoming clear that my job was coming to an end. I was in a weak state due to stress and had become dispirited. For a while, due to church politics, I had been particularly vulnerable through not having had much support from fellow Christians. It was a time when quite a lot of people had influenza and I developed a severe infection in my lungs. I took antibiotics and tried to muddle through all the emotional issues as best I could and I slowly improved. By the grace of God I moved to a new and better job. Some time later I tripped on the curb and severely sprained my ankle after being cursed by a beggar, to whom I had not given any money. A month or two later I developed the most terrible toothache I have ever had in my life, which was only relieved by having the tooth pulled out urgently at the dentist's. Then, some weeks later, I developed dysentery, probably from eating some badly cooked fast food. The usual medicines did not work and I only recovered after forgiving the church and calling elders to pray over me and anoint me with oil, as we are told to do in James 5:14. Subsequently, I recognised both an inherited tendency to become dispirited in this sort of way and also a failure to forgive myself after having accepted the Lord's forgiveness for sin way back in the past, and a consequent burden of guilt which was causing me to try to assuage it with stressful good works. I dealt with these issues spiritually before God; and I confessed to God that I had not dealt righteously with difficulties at work, and I sought forgiveness in the name of Jesus.

The opposition to Christianity in the workplace is increasing and many Christians work in complex environments where they suffer oppression that is subtle but severe. It helps to stand together in love with other Christians, confessing to one another and praying for one another, even when we do not understand each other very well, in order to overcome in the name of Jesus, and in order faithfully to bring in what He is doing (Psalm 133, James 5:16). We are weaker if we fail to stand together.

My spiritual defences had been particularly weakened when I had allowed stress and dispiritedness to get the better of my soul. Consequently my bodily defences had also been weakened and my breathing was attacked by prevailing infectious agents, because dispiritedness relates to the spirit retained from the air breathed in and the naturally acquired response to it, and my lungs were the weak point. Later, the weakened defences for my eating and excreting were similarly attacked. The whole episode was aggravated by being cursed and by not having recognised the fact quickly enough. I did not deal adequately with the spiritual issues at the time and consequently I became physically ill. The parts of my body affected were relevant to my inability inwardly to digest what was happening to me because of the extent to which I was not right with God. My weaknesses occurred at the points of conflict in my body:dispiritedness affected the lungs; excesses of wrong foods for false comfort affected the gut.

Protection

It is noteworthy that I was helped by finding a metaphor appropriate to my condition. When, by the grace of God, I found the word "dispirited" my healing opened up.

You can reach a point in your life where you may become ill unless you explain your difficulties to the Lord and allow Him to change you. Quite wonderfully, He helps you find the right words for your confession. He will always make available the small gate and narrow road that leads to life, which will always accord with His word; but it is so very easy in this world to avoid repentance, by finding reasons why it need not be applied to your suffering, and thus to justify yourself falsely. The world will always supply plenty of excuses for you and it is easy simply to choose a logical pathway that feels good that will nevertheless eventually end up in sickness.

It is necessary to know how to find the Lord's guidance when we are ill and it certainly helps to be in fellowship with other Christians who have tackled similar issues in themselves. If we are honest we shall admit that time and again and day by day we fail to realise all the implications of all we are doing, fail to take full account of the intricacies of all that motivates and affects us, and fail to acknowledge before the Lord that we are not truly free. He can often reveal such things to us; most easily through the help of other people who love us in the Lord and who are truthful with us and will wait on Him and pray with us. When stumbling blocks are present but unseen, all is not as well as it may appear to be on the surface and our spirits, souls and bodies may reflect the fact. Our weaknesses may be obvious to our Christian friends before they are obvious to us, so it helps to belong to a Christian community in which it is safe to be vulnerable one with another.

Every illness is essentially a spiritual problem and, although it may be entirely reasonable to seek a physical and technological remedy, we neglect the spiritual issues at our peril. They will inevitably recur, and may cause illness of various manifestations, until they are brought to God for healing in the name of the Lord Jesus Christ. We have a responsibility before God both to help each other in this respect (Galatians 6:2) and also to be accountable and responsible for ourselves in these matters (Romans 14:12, Galatians 6:5). The Holy Spirit will enable us to change by leading and discipling us through the illness, and all that relates to it, if we allow Him to do so (Hebrews 12:1–14) with the help of other people. Of course, illness is not from God. It is part of the human condition, and God knows it, and He will bring us through and change us and heal us so that we develop immunity to whatever attacked us. Just as we may gain immunity from infections we have had or have been innoculated against, like measles, so this may give us particular experience and resilience in certain respects which are useful to Him.

Sick society

The personalities and characters of gods are pervasively influential, begetting unconscious conformity to their image in anyone who offers them worship in any way. So relationships and behaviours in communities generally tend to adjust to whichever god is publicly worshipped and will tend to assume the nature of that god.

Religions have always involved themselves in health and healing. The agent of healing is spiritual and actual healing is divine (Isaiah 53 and 26:16–19). The ability to achieve a state of public health that is acceptable to the population demands a collective willingness to adopt changes which accord with whomsoever the majority really worship. Sophisticated technological cultures mostly look automatically and unconsciously to the gods of humanism.

When whole societies are wrong with the God of Abraham they cease to come under His blessing and consequently they become weak and, in the long term, fail to prosper. But most technologically sophisticated societies and communities are a long way from comprehending the spiritual factors which could cause their decline. Very few societies have realised collectively that Jesus can heal whole communities and nations.

Consequently individual Christians, and groups of Christians, are appointed by God to be His salt and light in societies whose ethos is generally opposed to them. Both our adversities and our illnesses may be used to discipline and change us personally so that He may be more revealed in our individual and collective lives. Then He may influence other people through us and we may intercede for them and to do the good works He wants us to do. Thus God's changes may be brought into the lives of other individuals and His kingdom may be extended (Matthew 5:13–16, James 2:17).

As we suffer and allow ourselves to change personally, under the hand of God, listening with humble hearts and minds to His direction, we may be touched with occasional miracles. Certainly we should expect them because God's power is inevitably at work in His people who are committed to Him, and His hand is upon them.

The germs and antecedent factors which form the basis of the scientific aetiology and pathogenesis of illness are generally found all over the place most of the time. In general it is reasonable to ask why they should be able to overcome your natural resistance in a certain place and at a certain time and to ask, "What part have I played and what has been going on for me to be suffering this particular illness just now? Why should this part of my body be a weak point through which illness could enter? Why should I have become so susceptible to this common parasite as to have allowed it to have gained a dangerous advantage over me?" These questions prove worthy of investigation although the appropriate means of investigation are not scientific but spiritual, relational and revelational. In order to answer them you have to look inside yourself and open your heart to what is truly going on there and seek God's wisdom with repentance.

It may take time to make adequate repentance this way. You should not expect to be able quickly to abstract yourself from such questions in order to give a simple answer to them. You can only tell your true story in your own time, with God's help.

And if you allow His Spirit of Truth to penetrate your heart, change your mind and direct your confession, and allow this Holy Spirit to reveal to you aspects of your body and soul and relationships which you may have preferred not to discover, you will find healing.

Epidemics are rather different because of the acuteness of the assault and threat they pose. Admittedly, during an epidemic of influenza, for example, when many people around you have influenza, your personal chances of catching influenza are markedly increased just by the proximity of other cases. Whether you like it or not you are at risk of suffering with the rest of the people amongst whom you are living.

In Europe, before significant increases in trade and war and urban populations, the children would all have been naturally challenged very early in their lives by endemic measles, mumps, rubella, whooping cough, chickenpox, diphtheria and poliomyelitis. Many would have had subclinical infections but there was a higher mortality and morbidity in those days, particularly amongst children, than would be accepted today. Those who survived would have had a naturally acquired immunity that would have made them strongly resilient to the threat of further infections. But as displaced people congregated in large numbers in towns and cities these infections, and others, for example tuberculosis, typhus, syphilis, caused harrowing distress and wretched death particularly amongst the poor. By God's grace public sanitary measures were developed in order to try to control all the disease. Today infection is artificially restrained by sophisticated public health and social planning measures for avoiding overcrowding, filth and squalor and by immunisation. It is probable that different epidemics would periodically afflict various societies much more often than they do at present if the immunisation of children had not been generally accepted. Smallpox seems to have been eradicated by such measures, although not so very long ago it used to spread periodically through most societies.

Throughout history malaria has been endemic in societies close to warm, marshy areas and it is still the biggest killer of all despite brilliant efforts at eradication. Tuberculosis still spreads easily amongst dispirited, overcrowded people despite years of scientific research and sophisticated drugs. For centuries plague has periodically spread through human populations exposed to increases of the rodent population, which lives on waste, and it has killed many people. And typhus has spread through those who live in dirty, overcrowded places and carry lice. AIDS is spreading so hugely that reporting is subdued for fear of spreading alarm. There are really no drugs to kill any influenza virus and virulent strains have occasionally killed large numbers of people in a short space of time.

God's displeasure with a whole society is recognised in the Bible as a basic cause of epidemics of "plague". Nowadays epidemics of other diseases should no doubt be included. The account in 1 Samuel 5 of the plague which spread from Ashdod, after the ark of the covenant had been captured, bears similarities to the history of the black death which ravaged Europe in the middle of the fourteenth century, at a time of terrible persecution of true Christians and expanding trade, and it also bears similarities to the history of the great plague in England in 1665, after the persecution of Puritans by the Cavalier Parliament.

You could say that whether or not you get ill depends on your way of life, both personally and collectively. You are more likely to be healthy if you maintain a loving and obedient relationship with God, together with others, in Jesus. What is going on is likely to be least noxious when right with God. This is not to say Christians will not get ill; they do get ill because they are members of fallen humanity in a fallen world. But Christians have the assurance that they are agents of His will and their souls are being perfected through what they suffer provided they listen very carefully to the Holy Spirit. They know they are salt and light wherever God has placed them. Despite their suffering, and even if they do not find healing in this world, they will in due course assume the place prepared for them eternally with Jesus provided they stay reconciled with Him.

Without the work and influence of individual Christians, and of small Christian communities, no matter how weak, infectious diseases and all the other ills of godless society would wreak much more havoc than they do. People who do not walk with Jesus do not live together in a way which is ultimately conducive to health. However nice and beautiful they may seem to be, and however healthy their lifestyles and their foods, and however effective disease prevention methods advised by medical science may be reckoned to be, if God is ignored disease or trouble will come some way or other. Advances in scientific genetics are useful for reproductive counselling but they will not prevent the sins of the ancestors and parents from being passed into the next generation of people some way or other. Immunisation may avert epidemics but collective sin will always beget some other devastation. The only person who can break the deadly cycle of degenerate cause and effect is the Lord Jesus Christ, through whom sins may be forgiven and demons cast out and their results, and societies, healed.

Unwholesome relationships

In the light of God, illness may result not simply from ignoring Him and rebelling against His word, both individually and collectively, but also from the other wrong relationships which ensue. The wounds which result from our relationships being wrong with God allow demons to influence and grip our souls. Wrong worship and failure to hear the truth of God's word, and to apply it according to His direction, cause trouble not only for individuals but for groups of people, too.

Relationships which go wrong, or which are wrongly made, wound the soul; and demon spirits invade those wounds and affect the personality just as bacteria and other parasites infect physical wounds. Furthermore, physical wounds are more likely when relationships are wrong with God, not only through accidents or violence but also as a result of misuse of the body when the human spirit rather than the Holy Spirit takes control.

There are agents all about us, both spiritual and physical, with the capacity to destroy. They gain access at the weak points and whether or not they can overcome us, and to what extent, depends upon our resilience, which is a function of our physical health, which in turn is a function of our spiritual health (namely the extent to which we love the Lord our God with all our heart, soul, mind and strength, and consequently humbly allow Him to change us, and to which we love our neighbours as ourselves). In other words, when our relationships are right with God we are most likely to be free of illness.

I remember a young girl who was brought to me by her mother because she seemed to be passing too much urine. When I enquired about the circumstances I discovered that the symptoms had started just after her mother and father had had a violent fight and her father had taken his belongings and left home. She had been deeply shocked, torn apart because she loved both her parents, frightened and rejected all in a very short space of time. She had had a stomach ache during all the disturbance. I found too much sugar in her urine and in her blood. She had suddenly become unable to metabolise or inwardly digest any sweetness. The local hospital confirmed that she had suddenly developed diabetes.

It is noteworthy that any sort of troublesome rejection is quite often felt physically somewhere around the navel, where the cord was cut after birth. Whenever someone gets stomach ache, like that girl did, or any other sudden illness, it is always worth carefully enquiring about what else may have been happening then. The context is always relevant and illness will usually be found to be associated with what was going on in significant relationships, as seen in the light of God. Putting things right with God as soon as possible may be surprisingly healing.

It is even better to do this late than never to do it at all. I remember a middle-aged man with severe chronic diabetes whose need for insulin was greatly reduced by sorting his life out with God, forgiving and being forgiven, and so on, many years after it began.

Whether there is only a mild gastritis or colic, or a serious duodenal ulcer, a dangerous appendicitis or a heart attack, or some other illness, healing will proceed much more smoothly if the spiritual issues are dealt with before God. And the sooner the better. Spiritual healing should continue at the same time as any medical or surgical treatment if at all possible.

However, if healing has to be sought for complex relationships it usually takes time. Whatever rejection there may be will involve forgiveness, which is often difficult. Sin needs to be remembered, confessed, renounced and forgiven. Natural human reactions, such as fear, insecurity, shock and other powerful responses need to be confessed as sin and the people involved in inflicting the wounds need to be forgiven. Then the Lord should be asked for His healing for every detail.

Even after medical or surgical treatment, if God's healing is not sought in this sort of way the spiritual and relational difficulties will remain to cause further distress and illness. Old patterns of behaviour continue until the soul is healed and changed by becoming reconciled to God. Demons of rejection and bitterness, of hurt and anger, and suchlike, may continue to afflict the soul until it dawns that it is possible to be set free from them in the name of Jesus.

Most medical professionals approach their work exclusively through science and most do not realise that disease may be associated with spiritual issues, or with relationships which are wrong in the sight of God. However, there are some others who are, indeed, aware of spiritual connections with illness but who offer spiritual pathways for healing that do not belong to the one true God. Ways other than that of the Lord Jesus Christ of Nazareth will lead to other trouble in due course because they will not be in accord with our maker's instructions. Furthermore, any approach to healing which involves attention to spiritual issues will inevitably also involve some degree of personal relationship with the person attending to your condition, and accepting that person's influence. So whom can you trust?

Location and nature of illness

The spiritual reasons why a particular part of the body may be affected in a particular way are worth considering. Whether or not the sin, the wound, the bondage or the unclean spirit, will affect the duodenum or the heart, or some other organ, may seem like a lottery until we realise that the various parts of our bodies have different functions that are both physical and relational (that is spiritual). They therefore have different meanings and relevance, which are incorporated together into our whole person, body, soul and spirit (1 Corinthians 12:12). No part, whether physical, biochemical or spiritual, may in truth be considered as disconnected from all the others.

The common use of words for bodily parts is of significance in this respect because the sense of hundreds of years of their use is likely to have some profundity. For example, the stomach is involved in comforting yourself with food but also with what you cannot stomach. Thus indignation may indeed make you sick.

The gut is involved with the digestion and assimilation of food, and with the courage necessary to meet challenges with guts. So what you cannot stomach may lead to a violent gut reaction of one sort or another. Other gut feelings, like anxiety, about what else you may have to take in besides nourishment, may become associated with the actual food and cause intolerance of certain foods. However, you will have the guts to face the world with courage and strength when you remain innocent but shrewd and are able by His grace inwardly to digest whatever God leads you into, when you have assimilated past experience with the help of His wisdom and when you know His peace in your soul.

The large bowel and rectum are concerned with collecting waste, which is to be disposed of in an appropriate place. The old Bible speaks of the bowels being troubled for other people, and of "bowels of mercies", implying that compassion and mercy may modify the gut reaction when the Holy Spirit lives within us. Living in the Lord transforms our natural reactions into His actions.

Furthermore, in Yorkshire I have heard the expression, "Don't cry in your gut," which, although it means "Don't give yourself gut trouble, or any other sort of trouble, because of another person," also cynically recognises the connection between our relationships and our personal physical condition. Those who would harden themselves against any sort of empathy with another person live only to exploit others. I prefer Henry Maudsley's dictum, "The sorrow which has no vent in tears may make other organs weep," which indicates that if the gut reaction of sorrow and concern is suppressed and given no expression, not even in faithful intercession, it may cause some degree of illness, like the weeping of diarrhoea in the gut or the weeping of eczema in the skin.

Other people may make us ill if we hold on to unholy reactions to them. So what should we do about it? The question pertains to our own health.

The heart is involved in the affairs of the heart. The kidneys are involved with maintaining sufficient biochemical balance to maintain the integrity of the living body, that is with the physiology of restraint. The brain is involved with the regulation of behaviour. The prostate gland and the womb are involved with sexuality. The skin is connected with modesty. The breasts with comforting a child and femininity. And so on. And all are interconnected.

Whichever organ turns out to have the weakness that singles it out for attack depends not only on the relation of the nature of the threat to the function of the organ but also on the general health of each other relevant organ and the way the person habitually responds to the sort of threat posed, which in turn will depend upon the extent to which every aspect of the spirit, soul and body has been reconciled to God. Disturbing dreams and preoccupation with fantasy of one sort or another are indications that related aspects of one's soul are not at peace and the bodily organs associated with the dream or fantasy will be the ones most likely to be affected with illness: the sexual organs with sexual fantasy; muscles and backbone with violent fantasy; kidneys with subtle fears and imbalances; the brain with doing things in your own strength; the heart with concerns and fantasies about attachment and love, and so on.

Moreover, the natural emotional responses to situations which arise in everyday living may show up a particular tendency for a bodily organ to react in a particular way. For example, anxiety and aggression may constrain the motility of the gut and cause ulcers in the upper part (gastric or duodenal ulcer) or in the lower part (ulcerative colitis) or absolutely stop a person eating (anorexia). The way a particular organ reacts to a set of circumstances depends on the extent to which all the desires and thinking patterns, including fantasies, and feelings associated with that particular organ in the past and in the present, have been reconciled to God.

Events may have happened in the past which seem to have been put out of mind but a certain set of present circumstances may bring the memory back, or may unconsciously threaten to do so, and this can sometimes cause great anxiety. In this situation it certainly helps to allow oneself to become aware of what the organ may effectively be remembering by reacting with symptoms in the way it does. It may well be discovered that something relevant happened in the past that has not been put right with God. Bringing it to light and being reconciled to God through Jesus can be healing.

Although we may quite frequently find that we have not developed the relevant awareness until chronic changes have set in, so that in the natural it seems too late for much physiological healing, we should not be afraid to approach sensitive issues. Embarrassment should never be allowed to get in the way. Miracles happen even in the severest chronic illnesses.

Weak points

Georg Groddeck, a German physician, psychoanalyst and colleague of Sigmund Freud, recorded a case in which a man had slowly become blind. The doctor had wondered what it might have been that the man had not been able to bear to see. With patience it transpired that the blindness had come on after he had cursed God for his misfortunes in front of a crucifix in the village square. When this was remembered, the man suddenly saw the reality of Jesus and confessed his sin and sought forgiveness, and the issues which created the blindness were forgiven, and the damage from the retinal bleeding was spontaneously absorbed and his sight returned.

Similarly, a lady developed ulcerative colitis at a time when she lied to try to avoid impending bankruptcy and save her marriage. Her pressing problems were intense. Urgent medical treatment was started with the help of the local hospital. However, by the grace of God it became possible over a period of time to recall, in connection with her illness, that from earliest childhood she had never been able to share significant distress and wretchedness with her mother. The mother had been unable to tolerate her child's expressions of distress or mess because she was constantly suppressing her own distress and mess about the insecurities and worries of her own life. Consequently the child had become intensely clean, and often constipated, so as not to upset her. Toilet training had happened too soon. For days the girl had not been able to take food easily due to constipation pains. She recalled that she had loved her mother dearly but had striven in her own life not to make the same mistakes she thought her mother had made. However, she realised that she had always lived with a lot of fear and insecurity. Her release came when she was able to get in touch with the consuming hatred she had for her mother, which of course conflicted terribly with the love she also had, and which therefore had had to be hidden and denied. As in childhood, her weak point was her bowels which had this time reacted to intense stresses, similar to those of her childhood, in a similar but worse way. Reconciling the past, and the hidden factors, with God, and discovering His mercy and applying it to her mother, eventually brought physical healing.

Sometimes demons get in through weak points in order to cause physical illness. Some physical illnesses are due to demonic agents and in order to find healing the demon must be commanded out in the name of Jesus and the weak entry point healed through putting the relevant issues right with God. The association of some cases of arthritis with unforgiveness, and with stubbornly standing one's justified ground, is quite well known. I have come across cases of asthma and other allergic illnesses which have been demonic. Cancers may be demonic and so may many other illnesses. Demons of anger and fear and worry and so on may also be present with the illness demon. These have no right to live in any body which belongs to Jesus so they should be commanded out in the name of Jesus, and they have to go.

A demon of asthma may get in at some moment when free movement of the diaphragm is stymied by panic, or some other emotion or suppression of emotion which, for a time, hinders the taking in of sufficient breath. And the demonic activity may be triggered though conditioning, often by pollen or by the droppings of the housedust mite, since these agents naturally cause some inflammation in the airways. As soon as you believe you have the illness you have received the curse of the diagnostic label. Curses stick until the person truly allows Jesus to become the curse instead, knowing He overcame it on the cross.

Furthermore, I remember a woman whose eczema (which is another allergic illness) left her when she gave birth and appeared instead in her baby. Just as that baby inherited eczema so all sorts of other diseases may be inherited. In such a case it is necessary ask God to heal the sins of the ancestors.

Being reconciled to God spiritually should be expected to affect our biochemistry and even our genes. Confessing our sin, our wounds, our bondages, our wrong attachments, our ancestors, and our demons, to God for reconciliation through Jesus allows His healing to come.

Living with illness

Of course, if you have not sorted yourself out with God before something really serious happens to your body you may just have to live as long as you can with physical problems. After all, getting yourself right with God is not the same as being right with the church or with other Christians, not the same as finding the right guru or church leader to follow and not the same as following all the right rules. The only way is a personal relationship with God, through the Holy Spirit and the Lord Jesus Christ, which gives living meaning and personal relevance to His word. Perhaps the closer we get to God the more likely we are to find healing but this requires the fear of God and the courage to be different, rather than the fear of people. Sadly to say, none of us seems to achieve this perfectly, which means that we can comfort each other with compassion through the loving comfort God gives to each one of us (2 Corinthians 1:3–11). But none of us can be at all sure that any serious illness will not afflict us.

To some extent we are all "in it" together. Some may have found more healing than others; some may be closer to the Lord than others but no one is exempt from suffering.

Your body is not disconnected from your soul, nor is your soul disconnected from your spirit and your spirit is not disconnected from other spiritual influences. What is and has been going on in your spirit may be reflected in your soul and what is and has been going on in your soul may be reflected in your body. You may have thorns in your flesh from living in this world and from your ancestors having lived in this world (Romans 8:18–23, 2 Corinthians 12:7) but "if the Spirit of him who raised Christ from the dead is living in you, he who raised Christ from the dead will also give life to your mortal bodies through his Spirit, who lives in you" (Romans 8:11).

The biggest question in all this is how to help people to be humble enough to look inside themselves truthfully and come before their loving, redeeming God in repentance to be reconciled and healed in Jesus' name. Maybe the only really effective way is for those of us whom the Lord Jesus has graciously changed to allow Him to continue to sort us out and heal us, so that He may be further revealed through us to others and be seen to dwell amongst us with salvation.

CHAPTER ELEVEN

MADNESS

Direction

Thoughts are revelations, inspirations, desires, enquiries, imaginations, developments with the benefit of memory and experience, reflections, deductions, anxieties. They come into the heart and are regulated by the brain, through which we become conscious of those that are relevant.

Thoughts come to us in response to what is going on for us, that is, in response to our reality, to where we perceive ourselves to stand in our relationships; and thoughts are allowed and accepted by us, and then taken and used, for their appropriateness. The path we may be pursuing depends upon the spiritual allegiance to which the heart is given; and our needs, desires and thoughts, and our consequent speech and behaviour, fall into line with it. If there is spiritual conflict, as there often is, there will be a certain amount of confusion.

Proverbs 27:19, says, "Just as water mirrors your face, so your face mirrors your heart". But what is in the heart is not always what we should like to be known. Although we may try to pretend with our faces, those with discernment will see through the pretence. In truth, we are not as we may pretend to be. We cannot altogether adjust what is in the heart to suit our cunning, although we may try to do so.

We should do well to avoid being ensnared in our hearts by evil. In Ecclesiastes 9:3 Solomon says, "The hearts of men are full of evil and there is madness in their hearts while they live." Jeremiah 17:9 says, "The heart is deceitful above all things and beyond cure." Jesus says, ". . . out of the overflow of the heart the mouth speaks" (Matthew 12:34). James 3:8 says, ". . . no man can tame the tongue." But there has been a cure for the heart since Jesus, and a control for the tongue. Through allowing ourselves to be reconciled to God when we suffer, our hearts become purified: "the blood of Jesus, His son, purifies us from all sin" (1 John 1:7). When we are baptised in His Spirit He becomes sealed within as our heart's treasure (Ephesians 1:13, Matthew 6:21) and then His Spirit is continually cleansing us from the heart. Nevertheless the purity of heart of each one of us is never perfect and some madness or other is usually there whilst we live in this world. It is part of our fallen nature.

The Bible tells us in several places that God knows our hearts (see especially Hebrews 4:13). Jesus knew what was in a person (John 2:25). Furthermore, we are told in John 14 that we should not let our hearts be troubled and that Jesus is the way, the truth and the life. That is, personal relationship with Him and trusting in Him, will bring us into truth and abundant eternal life. So, ultimately, all other ways, including any face we may put on to try to hide what is in the heart, are dead ends. Therefore our hope for sanity and healing and salvation lies in opening our hearts to him no matter what may be there and no matter what situation we may be in.

The word of God implies that any path other than that of Jesus may lead to madness in which sound judgement and sometimes self-control become lost. So it behoves us to consider all we do with sober judgement and only to become involved with what God gives us faith for (Romans 12:3). If we involve ourselves with good ideas which are not right with God,

we may find ourselves travelling down a road which may ultimately lead us towards madness through losing touch with His
true reality.

In common with all mankind, there have been moments when
I have personally been dangerously silly, when I have lacked
sound judgement, when I have felt utterly lost, insightless and
hopeless; and I do not find it difficult to imagine how such
moments could have become much worse. I was demonised for
years. I am not proud of all that. But I am redeemed and saved
and healed by the Lord Jesus.

So how can I call anyone mad just because they seem to have
gone wrong, or seem to be messed up and deluded, or because
that person's thoughts seem silly, confused or mistaken –
except, of course, in the heat of the moment as a gut reaction if
they really hurt me? With the help of the Holy Spirit who leads
us into all truth, I would rather listen to such a person, paying
close attention with the empathy of one who knows from
experience fairly well what they are talking about.

Perhaps that person may come to know that I know to some
extent, and feel truly heard enough to find their way. Likewise
I may come to know that person knows I know so we move on
in relationship. In this way people who are lost or stuck may
become able move on through whatever they have to go
through. Real relationship with someone else who has compassion, with whom it is possible to approach truth and try to make
sense, can lead towards healing in this sort of way. Issues may
be clarified and perhaps the Lord may influence the thoughts
and give revelation as personal changes come about through
the relationship.

People working through tough issues may find benefit from
regular times of meeting, once or twice a week, or so, over an
extended period of time. When they can trust that they will
be met faithfully and truthfully at the same time next week
issues come up from hidden unconscious places in anticipation
of the meeting and it can become safer to take the next step.

God expects those who listen to each other to be "clothed with compassion, kindness, humility, gentleness and patience" (Colossians 3:12) and He knows there are many who easily lose hope when they can find no-one to take them seriously and stay with them patiently and faithfully.

But I cannot make that person receive Jesus, although I know Jesus is the saviour of the whole world. Nevertheless if that person will, of their own volition, call on the name of the Lord Jesus Christ of Nazareth He will open their eyes and ears to what they cannot see or hear and will reveal Himself to them. But I cannot absolutely ensure that they do so. We are together in a mad and fallen world and I know there is only one small narrow gate out of it (Matthew 7:14) but most people do not seem to believe it is there. Sadly, the majority will choose any bolt-hole they can see when the going gets rough, and so they often get lost. We so easily go astray like lost sheep (Psalm 119:176).

Stigma

There is a stigma attached to the word "mad" which implies not only hurtfulness (that is, being wounding both to other people and oneself) but also being beyond the pale and excluded from what is going on amongst people who are significant.

There is another stigma, too, which serves as an euphemism covering up the truth of some uncomfortable aspects of a person's experience and condition, namely the stigma of being called ill. If you say someone is ill it may sometimes give you an excuse to treat them mercifully when you do not feel like it and when compassion is lacking in some respects, which amounts to condescension. A needy person, having given up hope of any possibility of being met in the light with true kindness, free of condescension and collusion, may become resigned to being treated with pity and to receiving charity. But to be categorised in this way, and treated without real empathy, will enable that person to avoid being truly accountable. However, every one of us is sooner or later accountable to God for all we do and say and no one is excused on account of illness of mind or body. There is no mention in the Bible of such exoneration.

To attend personally to those deemed mad or ill in order to try to help them truthfully to discover the meaning of what is going on for them must, therefore, tend towards healing. Such help would encourage them to move away from being stuck with a diagnostic label and enable them to begin to be accountable to God.

It is becoming fashionable to consider people who commit serious crimes to be ill, too. Commonly people say, "He must have something wrong with him to have done something like that!" Where there has been no death penalty for a few decades people have needed some excuse in order to allow themselves to develop some sort of understanding of those they secretly wish they did not have to keep alive. Since the reasons for criminal activity seem obscure to many people, psychiatric and psychological opinion is often sought, which invokes a possibility of illness.

A particular trouble arises from the fact that designating someone as ill carries a common implication that medical science, or its partners psychological science and nursing science, should manage them. The fact is that to be diagnosed as mentally ill or criminal, and to be managed scientifically, impersonally and thus without having to be fully and truly accountable, may bring enormous relief to the person so diagnosed. It may not only let them off the hook by seeming to provide a label, by way of diagnosis, as an excuse for their behaviour but it may also relieve their distress and sometimes save their lives. It also satisfies politicians and others who want to see something done about the perceived problem. But it easily obscures the consequences of those people, so diagnosed, thereafter being controlled by science and its politics, which can divert attention from their real healing and salvation. They will effectively become prisoners of the prevailing cultural system, often without knowing it.

Of course, people who offend persistently against the prevailing culture will inevitably be confronted with its legal sanctions and leave themselves open to being managed and having things done to them contrary to their will. Labelling and classification will assist the administration of the system's various agencies. But the diagnosis given thereby should not be assumed to contain the Godly truth of what is really going on. Neither science nor politics yield spiritual truth about the state of a person's heart or mind or relationships.

So it is foolhardy to offend against any cultural system to such an extent as to risk being labelled mad or criminal. There is no need for actual rebellion when Jesus provides the way (Romans 13).

Who to turn to?

The most important issue, however, is who to turn to when your world is falling apart, particularly if you seem to be out of your mind and rejected and desperately want to find healing and peace. What do you do in such circumstances when you do not know what to do? The administrative system of a supposedly civilised society is present with its many well-qualified employees, who often seem very nice and who may sometimes be genuine, and surely in this day and age there must be some technological relief for the torment you seem unable to escape from. The Christian church is not far away, but they may in practice, sadly, often seem too cosy in the confines of their religion and too unaware to understand the utter devastation of some human experiences or to have real faith for how Jesus could help. There are other religions, too, and some of them may seem interesting.

So is it just going to be a matter of finding some relief or is it possible somewhere to discover true healing? And if there is to be healing what has to happen? Is truthfully unburdening your heart of any relevance? In any case, is there anyone to talk to? Is being taken seriously going to change things? Can the human heart really become free of its madness and the human brain of its pain through some sort of relationship? Is it ever possible to get free and still remain alive?

One person in ten in sophisticated western societies is at some time in their lives diagnosed as having some sort of mental illness and at least one person in four has taken psychotropic drugs for some sort of madness when they have felt unable to contain it any other way. Such is the incidence of distress, in the realms of thought, feeling and behaviour, which is being covered up by sophisticated pharmacology, together with clever manipulation of the mind by the science of psychology and the social indoctrination of television. All this is a measure of the degree of unbelief in our so-called Christian societies.

If you turn to Jesus in order to be free it is necessary to realise that sticking to Jesus is not the same as trusting the church. And since rejection and exclusion from the society of people who are personally significant is often a very basic issue, it is certainly best to find one or two relevant people who will be real with you, people who are not judgmental, even when you are rough, who will faithful and patient and do you no harm. Sadly the people able to be good enough will not always be Christians.

Finding such people can be so difficult that you may be tempted to give up on such a quest and may even start to feel yet more rejected and resentful and hopeless. You may never have had the experience of talking to anyone who understands without judging and blaming you. So you may even be tempted into blanket retaliation against everyone, rejecting the whole apparently normal society in which it seems impossible to be taken seriously.

Regrettably, this is the origin of many a crime and many an incarceration and much violence and hopelessness. People naturally react and retaliate when there seems no other way of making the pain less. Anger and violence, for example, may seem to give some relief by expressing the pain. But such relief is always only temporary. Only later is it sometimes realised that dumping the emotions in retaliation does not actually make the pain less in the long run but rather perpetuates the pain by inflicting it on others. It also makes it easier to react in the same way next time. Thus people become hopeless and defeated because there can seem to be no way out, no way of actually getting rid of the pain.

People in this mess need supernatural help. And whichever god you call on by name will meet you. So be sure to call on the Lord Jesus Christ of Nazareth because He is the only one who took the ultimate rap for you. On the cross He took your pain and He will give you the power to get rid of it because of His resurrection. The power by which He rose from the dead will enable you to overcome the consequences of your actions and end the deadly cycle of retaliation. He will lead you to repentance and a real change of heart if you accept Him and yield it all truthfully to Him. Faith in Him will always ultimately lead to true healing and eternal life.

Abyss

When people are confused and pained about what is going on, and unable to find any relief, they often put their trust simply in their natural reactions. If nothing else makes sense, the pain you feel can actually be something real to hold on to. Anger can seem to give you back some sort of identity. Sadness and grief can often be powerfully justified. Natural censorship of difficult or painful material can be used to deny or hypnotize away the painful truth. The alternative, alone with no one with you and no one with whom to try to be real and accountable, can seem like a terrifying abyss.

The trouble with trusting in natural reactions is that demon forces of pain, anger, confusion, unforgiveness, defeat, denial, and so on, may recognise their chance of capitalising on your weakness, and come to dwell in your soul. Then you cease to feel able to get rid of those powerful emotions and their associated strongholds in the mind, because they become compulsive and habitual, being triggered by situations similar to those through which the trouble started. These demons know you need them so they can be hard to get rid of. Sometimes they take you over so completely that they increase the confusion. So, for instance, the more angry you become, the more frightened, and the more frightened the more rejected, and the more rejected the more envious, and your perception becomes distorted and voices from those demons may give you commentary or instruction, adding to the torment. Everyday work and meeting people in shops and public transport become impossibly painful because you get treated like someone strange. People secretly curse you and you perceive it but you can make no real contact with them. You are excluded, and anyone you turn to for help just seems to manage you impersonally without really meeting you, and you let them. Rejected and alienated, you can easily come to feel worthless. You may even reach a state of allowing yourself to be abused just to try to feel real. Sexual abuse may even seem comforting for a moment. Drug abuse may temporarily seem to take you out of hell. You can also take on the role and identity of a mad person, unpredictable, rejected, having no real personal contact with anyone. You can allow the system to control your life, and perhaps fill you full of drugs that manipulate your behaviour or your mood, perhaps in return for food and shelter in one of their institutions. This way you can deny any desire to be responsible for yourself and deny the pain of having given up all hope of healing. So you may justify your rebellion.

Rebellion like this is, after all, a sign of fighting for your life, in a way. Although it is a sign of hope, however, it is not the way of peace. You may have an excuse for your habitually extravagant behaviour but you will be wounding other people and wounding yourself and wreaking a lot of destruction. So wake up, you sleeper! Come to Jesus and do not kill yourself or anyone else (Ephesians 5:14).

If you give up hope and take on the guise of some sort of crazy person and comply with the official diagnosis "ill and mad" (there are other more sophisticated euphemisms) you generally cease to belong amongst those who signify. So you become free to duck and dive away from their commonly accepted culture. Enigmatic language and prejudicial logic may be privately developed as you become skilled at dodging the dread realisation that no one understands you. Everything can be very confused, even your feelings. Natural reactions may find no validation. You are in a prison without walls from which there seems no escape. You may pick up on influences and events which may, or may not, really concern you, and be unable to tolerate the anxiety of not knowing what they truthfully mean, and therefore jump to premature conclusions without expecting any confirmation from other people. Confusion may come from other people not meeting you with any apparent truth or from you, yourself, not being receptive to any truth. Overcome by rejection, hopelessness, worthlessness, and all sorts of other natural emotions, your natural attempts, in spite of everything, to develop some sense of reality beget realisations which seem to make sense to you but which fail to be truly accepted by others. Sensations of being affected by influences which you understand, but no one else actually does, may add to your confusion. Although you may not realise it, you will have given up on the idea of having any truthful, real, good, kind, healing relationship with anyone.

Rejection, more than anything else, is what moves this pattern of events away from reality, and each deterioration is often initiated by cursing from either other people or oneself, which exacerbates that rejection. One way or another people naturally curse those they do not recognise as belonging to the prevailing cultural norms. So very many people diagnosed by the modern system as schizophrenic have been pushed into craziness by curses. Such cursing can stick and often precedes admission to hospital.

To find healing it is necessary to be willing to try to forgive and be forgiven then to find the courage to allow a relationship with someone genuine. Only God can change your heart in this respect, so please will you let him do it? The only way to come to Him is through the Lord Jesus Christ of Nazareth. Please appeal to him first. He says: "whoever seeks finds" (Luke 11:10). Many other people say there are all sorts of other ways (and some of them call themselves Christian) but I am following what the Bible says. In John 14:6 it tells how Jesus says, "No one comes to the Father except through me." That tallies with my experience, and I have seen a lot of this and have been around longer than most. He is the one who can break the chains that bind you and truly set you free because He became a curse instead of you and rose from the dead, having defeated the powers of the world, the flsh and the devil. But whoever you ask for by name will come to you. There are many higher powers and spiritual beings. So be sure to ask only for the Lord Jesus Christ of Nazareth.

Earliest experiences

Sometimes this sort of craziness develops in very young children. Relationships are disrupted and demonic forces attempt to take control. The child is prevented from meeting the mother in truth and knowing her in such a way as to receive her sense, and so fails to connect with the world in a way that makes sense to others. The cause of the disruption in relationships may sometimes be due to weakness associated with having been physically ill, perhaps occasionally due to illness or trouble of some sort in the womb before, or during, birth. Babies are far more likely to be profoundly affected in their minds by physical events because so much is growing so fast and they have not yet developed the resilience of having made sense of their world in much detail. So the damage from physical weakness and illness may need healing through prayer before they can be set free from their demons, especially demons of rejection, in the name of Jesus. Then the Holy Spirit may be invited to retore the relationship with the environment because God loves the world (John 3:16). Then the Holy Spirit can be, as it were, the child's mother and work through the mother to bring love and truth into the child's soul. The medical and allied professions call this sort of condition "autism". The early signs of the condition are sometimes missed because making meaningful contact with babies happens intuitively, rather than through language, and the adults responsible for the child can easily feel the most terrible false guilt, especially when professionals to whom they turn for help fail to understand. But of course science does not of itself yield spiritual insight.

So much is being learned so fast in the early years that relationship trauma in pregnancy and early childhood can lead to major character weakness in the child that may be well covered up with adaptations as the child grows up. The cover-up is usually very plausible until some repeated pattern of events unconsciously reminds the soul, in later life, of the early trauma. Then the person may break down. In fact people to whom a lot of difficult, bad, painful things have happened in early childhood, without healing, may have a lot of undisclosed weaknesses covered up by a lot of plausible adaptations which in truth do not really reveal the person's true character and which hinder the soundness of their maturity. Their personality will function in this world through many compromises, self-deceptions, justifications and demons, although the whole may hold together remarkably well until that person is confronted, through everyday circumstances, with the abyss they have unconsciously always been striving to avoid.

An extreme example seems necessary to make the case clearly. A baby was subjected to extreme cruelty by having been made to submit to the most terrifying and painful ordeals by the people to whom the child looked for survival. This was done to inculcate evil power. The torture was never admitted and was always denied by the people involved. It was always unspokenly demanded that everyday life was to be conducted as though the child had never endured any pain or trouble, otherwise there would be further ordeals for the child. Thus the child's experience was never overtly confirmed. Although the fear and torment were always present the true cause was never acknowledged. With time, the details of the torture became distorted in the child's mind. Many details had never seemed clear at all. But reminders of one sort or another periodically caused unexplained responses, especially withdrawal, terror, rage. The seeming impossibility of ever trusting anyone or of ever being able to have good things led to habitual thieving, which eventually resulted in prison sentences of increasing length. It seemed that life had to be conducted in the denial that anything terrible ever happened, except that signals that seemed to be associated with past terror periodically and automatically reinforced compliance through fear.

To the casual observer, a person brought up in this way may seem self-controlled and usually able to behave as other people require. Big trouble usually starts, however, when the person is challenged by the prospect of really loving and being loved in truth with true accountability. Whether the person is aware of the fact or not, the love of God in other people presents the prospect of healing, of unconditionally reciprocating, and consequently of being authentic in relationships and letting go of the false faces of apparent social acceptability learned through fear. But then nightmares start and the pain covered up for so long begins to be felt and very troublesome behaviour demands vigilance.

A whole new world will open up as love is allowed in; but it may not be without pain. It is like fingers that have been dead with cold coming painfully to life again in the warmth. The natural reactions to what was once suffered come to life, and sometimes they are violent. You need to find and stay close to one or two people who will keep unconditional faith with you.

Jesus will heal you through them. Commit yourself to Him.
Stand on His promises written in the Bible. It takes time. Stick
with Him. Despite all the feelings of unworthiness, grief, self-
pity, pain, fear, rage, that may seem to confuse or overwhelm
you, keep calling on Jesus. Believe His salvation even when
clamorous voices tell you He is lying. He went through hell to
save you. Confess your feelings and give them to Him, yield
them to Him, and ask for His Spirit to come into you and heal
you. Tell Him you are sorry for having held onto the pain for so
long and for never really having known what He could do
before. And I hope you find people with Jesus in them whom
you can believe in enough, who will allow you to make some
mistakes, like a child, so that you can renew your mind according to the word of God and reconstruct all you have ever
learned in a spirit of love rather than a spirit of fear. It usually
takes a long time but that is all right.

We may consider another example, too, which is not quite so
extreme, the case of a man, the youngest child of a mother who
had been quite unable to cope after war came and her husband
had had to go away to fight. She was not only terrified of imminent invasion but she also had to look after two elderly relatives
and four other children, and the youngest baby was just too
much. Then when her eldest son was killed in shameful circumstances the whole family was filled with silent, bitter grief
which never went away. Everyone tried to cope as best they
could. People tried to smile, and painful feelings were suppressed because times were hard for everybody. But that
youngest child grew up into manhood in an atmosphere of desperate anxiety and sadness. Quite often he had to be seen and
not heard. He could not make a mess. So whilst he was growing
up he could not ask enough questions about what was really
going on, especially about worrying things and about death. He
lacked the opportunity and encouragement necessary to learn
how to resolve problems through constructive play and talk, as
children like to do. He learned to swallow his feelings and he

never grew to understand other people very well. Later in life, after he had married, one of his young children developed cancer and slowly died. Then, suddenly, his intense grief and rage, bottled up for years, became exceedingly frightening and confusing to him and he found it impossible to cope with emotions which he had never previously known he had. But by the grace of God, he found someone with whom it was safe to bring his feelings into the light to begin to make sense of them. Gradually, over a long period of time, he first learned to allow himself to become aware of his natural feelings and all the associated thoughts (he said it was like coming alive) and then he became able to tell Jesus about them and receive His healing.

Thus the relationships in which a child is nurtured in the early years, when personal development is proceeding so fast and in such detail, beget a template of experience and expectation which affects future thought and behaviour profoundly. When early relationships are fraught with confusion and rejection, deception and violence, or with similar agony, wounds in the soul generate thoughts and behaviour which naturally tend to wound others until healing is found. Wounds from the earlier years affect thought and behaviour more widely and profoundly than wounds from later on because as we grow older we usually find enough security to handle the knocks more easily.

Depression and anxiety

Adverse circumstances, bad decisions, confusion, bad relationships and worship that is not right with God, and so on, come into the lives of all of us, often causing us surprising trouble and deception. In consequence it can sometimes be difficult to avoid being burdened and oppressed one way or another for reasons which may not at first be obvious. Sometimes we get habitually locked in to sadness or anxiety, or some other emotion, which may be deep and profound so that there seems no way out.

These emotions are always natural reactions and they are never truly mad, although the reasons for them may not be obvious. Although sometimes you may feel a long way from His presence, God knows what you are feeling. The secret of getting out of being stuck in them is to find the way out; and the way out was usually the way in. You have to go back over what happened in order to get you into this mess and then make new sense of it with Jesus. This time you talk to God as you go because He knows the truth and His nature is to heal. There are certainly occasions when it seems impossible do this alone, so it is often best to find someone you can trust to help. These sorts of issues are so common that it is sad that they are not more usually discussed when Christians meet together.

Furthermore, it usually takes time to overcome many of the griefs and difficulties that afflict us in this world. Burdens need to be chewed over and issues need to be worked through. Despondency and anxiety are, in fact, to be periodically expected. If they are denied or suppressed they will probably surface again later, for there is sure to be a reminder. And it is by no means always simple to find a way out. Christians should not always expect immediate miracles. Those matters that take longer to heal change the details of our lives and it is often the details that need changing.

The study of the biochemical changes in the body's physiology that have been found to be associated with different moods and mental states has been used to develop drugs which can artificially make the biochemistry more normal again. The use of these drugs may make the mood and state of mind normal enough for there to be no need to take time off work. But this does not tackle the root causes, which may remain.

We all get into various dire straits when the pressures from within and without become excessive. The oppression may come from either external circumstances or personal responses, and we may be unable to cope with either. Issues we cannot face breed trouble. Panic may sometimes set in when there seem to be too many powerful influences and no immediately obvious right direction.

Panic is a natural reaction to certain circumstances but it may become automatically, unconsciously associated with things, or patterns of events, connected with it. A person may inadvertently have learned to panic when a mouse or a spider or a snake is seen, or at the thought of social activities, and may thus become phobic. Or panic may become automatically associated with the idea that unless we do something or believe something or other, or behave in a certain way, something terrible will happen. This may rapidly become ritualistic so that we may be labelled obsessively compulsive. The devil is always ready to get into us and deceive us, particularly in our weak moments. Our weaknesses are often connected to unhealed wounds from the past. If we allow them to do so, panic demons or worthlessness demons or sadness demons, and so on, readily take any legitimate opportunity to try to control us and subtly destroy us.

When the demon is expelled in the name of Jesus, the memory often comes to mind of when it first got in, and past incidents can be healed.

Addiction

When plans and relationships go wrong we often seek comfort. At those times we may often behave as though we have never really been weaned from our mother's breast. We regress to proven comforts by way of sucking, one way or another, on anything that comes to hand. Some people inject. And the devil is expert at putting very destructive substances in your way just at those moments when you seem most to need them. Whatever offers immediate comfort may seem, for the moment, better than the pain of facing all that is wrong, particularly when no-one understands. When all hope has gone and when it has seemed impossible to find any safe space to suffer and fools expect you to be tough, you can learn to rely on an anaesthetic.

The human heart craves faithful loving relationship more than actual things, more than substances. But most of us learn, at some stage of our lives, how hard it is to believe that it may have been better to have loved and lost than never to have loved at all. I remember a lady coming to me for a repeat prescription for sleeping pills and commenting, "These are more reliable than a fella!"

But sooner or later the sting in the tail of the substances we crave becomes aggravating. The damage caused by our addiction becomes apparent and it is usually very severe. Then who is dependable and powerful enough to drive the demon out and replace him with love and healing? With whom can you fill the void? The Holy Spirit is the comforter, and He will fill you after you really repent and get baptised for the forgiveness of sins in the name of Jesus (Acts 2). Then healing comes, and new life. God wants us weaned of this world's addictions (Psalm 131).

Mania

Other people may seek to avoid intolerable emotions and oppression by speedy and ill-directed escape behaviour. In their flight from intolerable grief, dread, pain, rage, they refuse any comfort, believing none to be ever good enough. They reject everyone. They become ready to flee or fight at any moment, deceptively denying any accountability, refusing to accept any limits, before coming to the limits of their human strength and sinking into abject despondency. Mania like this, when all normal relationships are impossible and the adrenalin is running high, is dangerous. It is very necessary for those people who have been close to someone like this to protect themselves and protect their finances. Drastic action and emergency services are usually very necessary.

People who are manic or whose behaviour reveals that they have in fact lost all self-control and all ability to be responsible for themselves may become even more desperate if no one forcefully restrains or holds them. If they cannot be contained somehow within human society they dwell in a destructive wilderness like the Gadarene demoniac. There are ways of forcefully but non-violently holding them in a closed environment, usually with drugs. Such treatment is pragmatic but not in itself healing. How do you get through to them to bring them back into a world in which there is love and mercy, where we all get it wrong and there is forgiveness and their mess can be cleared up? Well, believe me, by the grace of God and with compassion it is possible.

Breakthroughs

The Gadarene madman met Jesus and was immediately healed (Luke 8). These days the hope is that relationship with other human beings may be good enough to hold someone whilst they heal. It works much better if people may meet Jesus in us. Even then none of us is perfect. I remember instances when it has been possible to break through to the real person against seemingly formidable odds. There needs to be some mercy, some ability to forgive on the part of each person, some mutual recognition of our common human vulnerability. The healing usually takes longer than it did with Jesus – unless you actually have the gumption to call on the Lord Jesus Christ when you are crazy and he reveals himself in power to you directly.

Surprisingly, although our desperate states are always tragic, to a greater or lesser degree we can sometimes admit, with hindsight and humility after we have met Jesus, that we may have actually needed our nervous breakdowns. If we have brought God into our suffering He will have used it to change us. We shall have matured to some degree. Through suffering what we could not in truth avoid, and by working through it all by the grace of God, we may come to realise that God has given us the motivation and direction for breakdown to be transformed into breakthrough.

I have known anxiety and depression to have been described, by some who have suffered and come through them, as similar in some ways to a pregnancy in which something that had been brewing was eventually brought to birth, resulting, by the grace of God, in realisations and events which were good, through which new strength, new life, hope and the peace of God were found.

Even if a person has been so extravagantly distressed as to have needed firm restraint, and even though strong sedatives may have been used, sometimes for a long time, the presence and direction of Jesus, working through His people, can lead that person out of it all into healing. If the drugs should interfere too much with true thinking and real feeling it may become possible, with the prescriber's agreement, to reduce the dose if it is safe enough to do so. It is best to keep in touch, and to keep faith, with someone to whom you can be fully accountable with whom you can talk and pray deeply. Usually it all takes time but it is worth it.

Through the guidance of the Holy Spirit what the world calls madness or mental illness becomes meaningful and accessible to God's healing. In this world very many knocks and bad experiences are to be expected and in general, if we discard wishful thinking and rose-coloured spectacles, it seems to be raw human nature to treat each other appallingly, despite many a pretence at being nice. In the absence of healing, bad experiences naturally cause bad reactions and produce bad thoughts and behaviours that wound people. Some of these thoughts and behaviours create serious wretchedness, often in a disguised way. The causes of unfaithfulness, violence, terrorism, rejection, robbery, constraints on freedom, madness, and so forth, lie in our human nature and the demonisation from which we fail to protect ourselves. Sadly, the root cause of the distress for which people frequently seek help usually puzzles them. Such is the hardness of the human heart.

The only person to make an eternal difference is Jesus, who softens and opens the heart and brings it alive. When he has come into a person's heart the effects are felt for many generations afterwards and those who remain His disciples live in His salvation for ever, both in this world and outside of time.

In the light of Jesus, the opposite of madness is not reason but freedom. Indeed, madness can often seem very logical once you get the hang of the logic. The freedom of salvation from the forces natural to this world is found only through the Lord Jesus Christ of Nazareth. He brings us into a spacious place (Psalms 18:19; 66:12) where there is peace. His is a spirit of power, of love and of a sound mind (2 Timothy 1:7) and where His Spirit dwells there is freedom (2 Corinthians 3:17).

CHAPTER TWELVE

HEALING

Faith

If you think of all the illnesses in the people you know, and of all the sicknesses you yourself have had, you will realise that the common state of mankind is to live with ill-health. It is hardly surprising, therefore, that by nature we should seek remedies wherever we can find them, and rely on our stock of tablets at home for our commonest complaints.

I practised medicine professionally for many years and long ago realised that, for best results, it is necessary to prescribe what a person believes in. A remedy is most likely to work if the patient believes in it. A remedy may be entirely appropriate but, if the patient does not believe in your prescription, often it will not work and the resulting annoyance may spoil relationships. Sometimes, of course, patients are somehow persuaded to believe in what you know they need rather than what they want. It has even been shown that the colour of the tablets can make people believe in them more. And occasionally tablets can be given which look authentic but which contain no active medicine at all, and they will work. This is called the "placebo" effect. So it is clear that faith is more powerful than science.

Secretly, I have always been astonished that anyone should believe that any chemical would ever bring actual healing. But I know that people do not usually think about healing and all they often want is relief. It has never been easy to shift the thinking of people, who normally attend a professional consultation expecting the medicine to be scientific, into thinking in terms of the holistic healing of their spirits, souls and bodies, which means getting their lives right with God through Jesus Christ. When someone is quite seriously ill, moreover, it usually does not help to call attention to the limits of scientific medicine. I well remember once trying to point a man in the direction of true healing and wholeness and being told: "Shut up, Doc; just give me the pills!"

True healing may sometimes be hard to find, even when you seek God for it with all your heart. Meanwhile drugs and medical treatments will usually make it possible to endure an illness more easily by curing some of the symptoms and thereby holding the person whilst some natural healing takes place. For disease of the physical body, selective drugs may be ingested into the body in order to kill the agents of disease rather than to kill the tissues of the body; symptoms may be removed to lessen the risk of hopelessness; biochemical abnormalities may be corrected; biochemical disease processes may be controlled; pus may be drained surgically or diseased parts of the body may be cut out, and so on. Directions may be given about rest and diet and exercise in relation to stress and to work.

As a splint holds a broken bone whilst it heals, so medical technology may be used to hold a person whilst some healing comes. Except in a few very extreme situations, and contrary to popular opinion, health and survival do not, however, absolutely depend on drugs or medical technology. Illnesses will quite often heal without drugs. About two thirds of cases of most diseases would improve with common sense and without any medical technology at all. Furthermore, the technology itself is not the agent of actual healing. Who knows, then, where healing comes from?

Very many people seem not to know what, or whom, to believe any more about anything, not just healing. The human reasoning currently fashionable in the field of education looks critically, but selectively, at every system of belief without making value judgements whilst many people who are privately cynical hold on to any system of thinking they fancy without considering it foundational. The only things apparently that seem real to many people are those abstract facts of science which seem to be proved statistically and those media personalities whose crafted images capture their fancy. Both are virtual in that they avoid the engagement of the whole person, spirit, soul and body, in any real relationship. Furthermore, we can never have a pure science of relationship because the necessary study would inevitably involve standing outside relationship. Science can describe the physiological and biochemical processes of healing but it cannot explain where the tendency to heal comes from. Looked at only scientifically, it is a wonder we are not all dead because of all the forces (ignorance, parasites, demons) ranged against us.

So there are many amateur philosophers and politicians, and many psychiatrists and psychologists, who reckon that healing is more likely to occur if we get our relationships right by taking full account of our human nature. The assumption is that it is not possible to change our nature. Therefore they attempt to give reasonable, justified expression to the diversity of human nature and to regulate human society through a democratic process. Getting clear, through discussion and debate, about where we stand with each other should then, they believe, enable us diligently to pursue reasonable mutual goodwill. In theory, human beings should be able to achieve some sort of equilibrium this way, so that healing would have the best chance. Stress is so prevalent that living more tolerantly with our neighbours, relatives and friends is bound to improve matters. But since powerful hidden agendas fail to come to light without the Spirit of Truth, what ultimately proves to count is who is worshipped.

Conversely, there are very many people who privately believe that relationships are never to be trusted because people will always let you down. Since most people have learned to be suspicious of other human beings, the notion of getting relationships right is, in fact, commonly extended into the spiritual dimension. The search for spiritual revelation, help and advantage is widespread. Although spiritual beings who do not have physical bodies are considered to be supernatural, the stuff of myth and fantasy and therefore unreal, they certainly generate great interest, and consequently they have real influence. Thus many people develop a relationship with one or more spiritual beings without realising that this is what they are really doing. In fact each one of us frequently considers with some intimate spiritual being those private matters that arise deep in the soul. We often talk things through in our hearts with a presence greater than ourselves. This may not be the Lord Jesus Christ, even though you may believe it is.

The diversity of spirituality in a society may add fanciful inclusiveness to public debate but it has hidden effects because the spiritual influences with whom we consider matters do, in fact, change our human nature. They make crucial aspects of our nature more like themselves. They change the operation of the censor, alter the processes of perception and cognition and consequently change systems of thought and behaviour and the nature of the society in which we live.

The only God to give the freedom of wholeness is the person whom Jesus Christ of Nazareth called Father. This is the God who made us in His own image. When we have His nature we are free, and healing is included in that freedom. If we genuinely love Him He is ultimately able to transform every aspect of our fallen nature into His nature through the power of His Holy Spirit. His Holy Spirit is received through repentance after we accept that His only begotten Son, Jesus Christ of Nazareth, died by crucifixion to pay the redemption price for our personal sin. Submission to God, in loving personal relationship with the Holy Spirit, and a life of continuing repentance, fully accepting the sacrifice of Himself which Jesus made, are essential for continued wholeness and healing.

Clearing rubbish

With reference to this one true God, the dictum credited to the sixteenth-century French physician and surgeon Ambroise Paré still holds good: "I tend them; God heals them." All good doctors use their science and their art to get rid of all that gets in the way of all the healing which God, by His grace, may give. Debridement is the technical term for this and it has been established for centuries as a basic principle of surgical practice.

In order to promote healing it is necessary to remove the dead tissue and the dirt, and the tissue which is too damaged to heal, and to tend the injured parts of the body with exquisite sensitivity to their viability. The work demands personal, professional, authoritative attendance and truthful, discerning attention from the physician or surgeon.

The surgical principle of debridement holds good for healing in general. It applies equally to the healing of body, soul and spirit. If what hinders healing is cleared away, healing may be expected by the grace of God.

God heals because it is His nature to do so. We may be healed through meeting Him. He is particularly to be found amongst His people, those who come together into the name of Jesus. We are more likely to be healed if we remove whatever gets in the way of meeting Him.

However, our fallen nature is such that it is only by the grace of God that we can properly perceive what needs clearing away and only by the wisdom and authority which come from being a disciple of His only begotten Son Jesus Christ that we can do it fully. Only by the influence of the Holy Spirit does it become adequately apparent that the healing of the body involves the soul and the spirit, that the healing of the soul involves relationships and that the healing of the spirit involves Jesus. It is not possible to find complete healing for one part without affecting all the others and all healing is essentially spiritual. In the words of Jesus (John 6:63) "The Spirit gives life; the flesh counts for nothing." After accepting Jesus and offering our bodies as living sacrifices to God (Romans 12:1) the Holy Spirit invites us to respond to God by seeking to be reconciled through Jesus, with repentance, which will affect every part of our being. Thus a process of healing may be expected to extend into every aspect of body and soul under the guidance and power of the Holy Spirit.

As our lives adopt more of God's nature, through the activity of the Holy Spirit living in us, whatever needs to be cleared away out of our lives becomes apparent. However, we do not see the full extent of the necessary debridement all at once but only what we need to deal with and get free from for the moment. The Holy Spirit leads us into healing step by step.

There is opposition. Old habits die hard. Everything about how you have been living up to this moment is the best adaptation to your circumstances hitherto that you have naturally been able to find. Even your illness may be seen in this light, although the fact that you have in one way or another become ill is what will have alerted you to the need for change. The Prince of this world and his demons want to deceive you into believing there is no real hope of radical change and that you should accept your fate.

It has occasionally been said that we both need and deserve our illnesses. Indeed, it can be instructive to try with God's help to work out why this may be the case. Often it is useful to begin with a truthful account of when the illness started and what connection there may be with whatever else was going on at that particular time. Healing demands real change and therefore real faith. Illness is a time of crisis. What is God saying to you?

First of all to be cleared away, there is *sin*, which is every response of the human organism which is not directed by the

Holy Spirit to be right with God. It is necessary to know God in a personal relationship and to become personally aware not only of His love but also of His justice, and consequently to know the peace and healing afforded by His law[1], in order to become aware of it. This personal relationship comes from turning to Jesus for salvation and accepting Him, accepting that on the cross He paid the price to redeem you. When you allow God to open your eyes it becomes apparent that sin leads to illness. The way out of sin is to submit your natural reactions to God for Him to transform them through the power of His Holy Spirit. Thus, for example your natural anger, in response to some perceived offence, may be given to Him (see Romans 12:19) and become transformed into forgiveness. When the Holy Spirit has lived in you for a long time this gradually becomes more automatic so that the Holy Spirit checks you when you go wrong and you are tuned in to hear and take note.

I am not going to write any list of sins. To do so could easily lead to legalism. Conviction and rescue are personal matters which arise from the activity of the Holy Spirit. This is particularly discussed in Romans 7. However, it is necessary to be aware that we can be burdened not only by our own sins but also by the sins of our ancestors (as in Exodus 20:5 and Deuteronomy 23:2) and that we may confess our ancestors' sins, as best we may, and be forgiven for them as well as our own (Ezekiel 18 and Luke 1:54–55).

Secondly to be cleared up and healed there are *wounds*. It is not only physical wounds which injure us, and through which infection and deformity may come, but also spiritual wounds through relationships which are wrong with God. These may often come about through no fault of our own as, for example, when a child is abandoned but they often lead to natural reactions which are wrong with God. For example, a person who

---

[1] God's law is a description of how it will be when we are right with Him.

was abandoned as a child may never trust anyone again and may consequently reject many people habitually. Thus wounds of the soul may persist and naturally lead us into behaviour which wounds others and is sinful. We may be so used to these aspects of our behaviour that we fail to be aware that they are wrong in the sight of God until we are suddenly convicted through the loving, healing work of the Holy Spirit. Healing comes through recognising the wound through which sin entered. It is necessary to discover the truth of what was going on, to forgive and be forgiven and to ask the Lord to heal and restore the body and soul and spirit. This is repentance and it can be painful and may involve suffering. If we are open to receive His healing and to allow ourselves to change He will bestow it and move us how and where He wants us to be.

The commonest wounds of the soul come from abandonment and loss, invasion of personal boundaries, curses and domination.

The loss of someone to whom a person is deeply attached can be worse than the loss of a limb. the wound goes deep and many demons can get in there. It is necessary to remember the past and put it right with God. It is essential to get to a place within yourself where it is possible both to begin to be willing to forgive and also to be able to receive God's forgiveness through confession. There is no point in carrying false or unnecessary guilt because that in itself can make a person ill. The truth sets us free but often we can only get to the truth through revelation from the Holy Spirit.

Violence, cruelty, abuse and rape are far more common than we like to believe and the trauma is enormous. The protective boundaries of the personality will have been severely breached and its integrity may have been shattered, and demonic influences will usually have entered the wounds. Sadly, the result will be harmful attachments to people and sinful responses, connected with the trauma but inflicted on many undeserving people, until the original trauma is healed.

The memory of such devastation is often deeply buried, only penetrating the surface of consciousness when a reminder penetrates the defences, which are firmly erected to prevent any remembrance. After any successful reminder there may be emotional turmoil, erratic behaviour and nightmares. Healing is often piecemeal, occurring in the disciple as the issues the Holy Spirit brings into consciousness are dealt with before God.

It is useful to have regular times of meeting in order to speak about yourself, letting issues come up from your heart, in a safe place at least once a week with someone you trust who will keep faith with you. Those regular times create an unconscious expectation, which the mind and heart automatically prepare for as the normal business of the week proceeds, so that more material may be healed in a shorter time and be adequately contained in the process. It is important to remember two things in particular: first, that a willingness to try to forgive usually precedes the ability to do so and, second, that there is usually a great deal of false guilt into which we need to ask the Lord to shed His light so that we may see the truth.

Although the old proverb says: "Sticks and stones may break my bones but words will never hurt me", this is only bluster because words wound worse. What is spoken soul to soul tells on us and takes its toll. The spirit in which something is said is given precision through the words of the tongue and may find its mark in someone else's weakness. What counts is the spirit in which words are spoken and Jesus said there would be a reckoning of words (Matthew 12:36–37). Even though a curse may seem to fall like water off a duck's back, it sticks. It penetrates thick skin to make it thicker and to make the heart harder. It is recalled at a moment of doubt to weaken resolve. It eats unconsciously into the soul to bring about its destructive intent.

Divine power, greater than human, is needed to overcome the effect of personally received words. The power of curses, wrong prayers and accusing tongues (Isaiah 54:17) may most powerfully be broken in the name of the Lord Jesus Christ of

Nazareth, because He became a curse for all of us (Galatians 3:13). After this fact is accepted and proclaimed (Romans 10:9) it is necessary, in order to be healed, to forgive and to bless those who have cursed you (Luke 6:28).

To be dominated is to be controlled through fear, fear of deprivation and loss, fear of abuse, fear of curses, fear of being manipulated into doing things before you can muster the wisdom and self-control to escape. Oppression like this bows the head, sallows the skin, and crushes and breaks the spirit, but so very often people take it for granted that it is natural to live like this. The wounds become manifest as rot in spirit, soul and body. If ever there should be a glimmer of light, portending release, a glimmer of the salvation offered through Jesus, the natural rebellion of our human nature may generate such revolutionary activity as to become brilliantly self-justifying and even violent. This in turn creates its own wounds, for our human nature alone can never bring release. It is necessary to develop a personal relationship with the Lord Jesus Christ in order to forgive and get free. With His Spirit there comes joy and peace and freedom in the soul (2 Corinthians 3:17). In fact people living in the freedom given through the Holy Spirit can even accept living as slaves or prisoners in this world (Ephesians 6:5–8).

Thirdly to be cleared up in the light of Jesus are relationships in which you are bound to another person by anything other than love expressed in a way which is right with God. *Bondages* occur whenever you make any commitment in relationship that registers in the heart, whether or not you allow yourself to be aware of the fact. Bondages ultimately sicken the soul unless there is peace with God about them. Such bondages tie you down and restrict your freedom, although you can be so accustomed to them that you fail to be aware of the encumbrance. Through people with whom you do not have peace you may be trapped; through people you have not forgiven you can be burdened with unforgiveness; through mistakes you can be burdened with guilt; through pacts and promises you can be bound to honour ungodly allegiances; through people with whom you have had sexual relations you can be subtly but powerfully influenced (note Numbers 25); through people with whom you have worshipped other gods you can be in bondage to demons; through not letting go of people when they die you can be open to demonic influence, too.

For healing to occur it is necessary for relationships, past and present, to be put right with God so that there are no longer any attachments that are not right in His sight, and so that His peace may come to your soul. This involves allowing the Holy Spirit to reveal the truth about relationships and to enable you to forgive and be forgiven, and to allow Jesus to take your guilt (which is iniquity, as in Isaiah 53). It involves using the authority given to you by the Holy Spirit to cut yourself off (as in Psalm 118:8–12) from people you were one in flesh with (as in 1 Corinthians 6:16), or with whom you were united in other ways, and asking the Lord to restore to you whatever you may have lost to them and heal you of what you took from them. When Jesus releases you, the unexpected freedom makes you realise just how much other people used to pull your strings.

Fourthly, and finally, it is necessary to be rid of *unclean spirits*. This, too, demands the authority which the Lord Jesus Christ of Nazareth gives to His disciples (Matthew 10:1 and 28:18–20). Unclean spirits, or demons, exert a control over a person's life in ways peculiar to the particular spirit, which a person may or may not be conscious of. So a demon causes you, to some extent and in some aspect of your life, to live for something other than Jesus. They have all sorts of characters and some are stronger than others.

There generally seems to be a particular time and place for any deliverance. The Holy Spirit works in the soul until conviction comes, often quite suddenly, occasionally with some extravagant manifestation of the demon. If simple confession of a sin and renunciation of it and acceptance of the Lord's forgiveness do not result in freedom, a demon may have to be commanded out in the name of Jesus by someone who is a disciple of Jesus – sometimes even by yourself. Demons are often expelled in the breath with a cough or a vomit. Who wants to be controlled by a demon? Get rid of them! If you have trouble with them you may need the help of others in the body of Christ. Jesus has equipped His church; although you may have to be shrewd and seek His guidance about whom to ask rather than simply asking the advice of a church's frontmen. One or two good books about deliverance are listed in the bibliography.[2]

Truth-speaking

We need the help of each other in the body of Christ. Where two or three have been led together by the Spirit of God into the name of Jesus, He is present (Matthew 18:19–20). Where the Spirit of the Lord is there is freedom (2 Corinthians 3:17) and He is the truth (John 14:6). His truth sets us free (John 8:32). So where His Spirit speaks through people who belong in His body (Colossians 1:17–18) we may receive truth which sets us free.

Truth is often not actually spoken with conscious intention; that is it does not come from human beings but from the Spirit of God speaking through human beings. It is present in what is going on, spoken personally by the Spirit into His people and revealed to receptive individuals. Not much truth comes into conversations that avoid reality, so it will not be found much in everyday pleasantries. It is more likely to be found through seeking God's face about those issues that cause discomfort. He knows what is going on for everyone and He always wants to heal. He loves each one of us so there is no need to be too sensitive or resistant to receive His word.

---

[2] The teaching about sins, wounds, bondages, and unclean spirits is that of The Order of Jacob's Well.

If truth is to be received for healing, love is necessary, unconditional love without bonds working through people who belong to Jesus. Not sentimental, sympathetic love but unconditional love which jealously longs for truthful accountability and bleeds at the lack of it (Luke 22:44) and intercedes. Eberhard Arnold said, "Truth without love kills; love without truth lies." Truth cannot be received by way of cold accusation but Godly love rejoices in truth (1 Corinthians 13:6).

It is not actually necessary to be a disciple in order to turn to Jesus for His healing. It is available for all (see Luke 17:11–19). His presence in the people who are true to Him evokes the necessary faith. Sadly, many Christians who give Him only nominal allegiance do not make Him king in every aspect of their lives, and often His Spirit is not active amongst them, despite their being called by His name. But where Jesus is truly known and His Spirit is alive and active in lordship anyone may be set free.

We are touched and convicted through His truth and released through His redemptive love in action. His presence, His truth and His love, have authority. The blood of our Lord Jesus, shed on the cross for us, has power over sin, over all the powers of this world, the flesh and the devil. Deception and accusation need no longer have any hold on us (Revelation 12: 9–10) and sickness is healed (Luke 7:18–23).

Conviction dawns from within. It is the work of His Spirit. The truth of it creates faith. We respond to the love of the One who made us in His image. Healing may sometimes be instantaneous but at other times a process of repentance begins, which will lead to various healings in due course.

I believe God always prefers His healing to be part of discipleship, drawing us ever closer to Him, and I believe that when someone becomes a true disciple healing continues as a process which lasts a lifetime, with occasional notable miracles now and then. Accepting healing thus becomes part of what the Bible calls holiness and what some people call sanctification

(Hebrews 12:10–14). Repentance is the process of submitting to God, as He makes His truth apparent, and humbling yourself so that He can raise you up (James 4:10) and purify you (1 John 1:8 – 2:2). For the disciple this becomes a way of life.

Containment

Sometimes, however, repentance can be quite a disturbing and distressing process and sadly the hospitality to be found amongst Christians may not always be as good as you need it to be. When what is significantly going on for a person cannot be held within available relationships, it is common to turn to psychiatry or psychology or philosophy. These disciplines are essentially abstractions, useful for administration but unable in themselves to lead you to the true source of healing. However, very many people who have never found the faith for healing amongst Christians resign themselves simply to accepting this world's systems of treatment and control of illness.

Psychiatry and psychology are generally controlled by administrations which are political, advancing the power of their profession, and generally unsympathetic to the processes of Christian discipleship. Their faith is in humanism, science and economics and their containment of disturbance tends to be utilitarian. This can sometimes hinder the Lord's healing. So they should be used only when trouble is so out of hand that their use seems imperative.

Some input from other believers, preferably from those who have trodden a path of repentance, healing and holiness in their own lives, often seems necessary, in the early days of disciple-ship, in order to substantiate revelation given by the Holy Spirit. It is particularly encouraging when other people who understand what is going on are generous and hospitable. Some sort of teaching, either through books or programmes or lectures or discussion groups, also helps to open eyes and ears (Isaiah 6:9–10). Jesus taught with unassuming authority and people usually seem to have been free to question Him and to engage in some repartee as He went along. He seems to have engaged in more intimate discussion with His close disciples. Teaching which is, in effect, sound interpretation of the Bible applicable to everyday life can effectively help to contain even the most distressing paths of repentance, and to bring healing, maturity and peace by building inner security, reducing fear and nurturing the capacity to love and be loved.

Without such teaching, natural reactions of the vulnerable soul, extravagant feelings, prejudices and doubts, easily get in the way of what God is doing. But if the teaching should err it is very easy for vulnerable people to be deceived. Didacticism carries the danger that people will follow the teacher legalistically rather than following the leading of the Holy Spirit within themselves. Jesus taught in parables that needed personal revelation from the Holy Spirit in order to be understood. So those who are taught should always be encouraged to criticise and question their teachers and to enter into some discussion with them, as people did with Jesus. And in order to keep safe they should keep on checking with the Bible what they are taught, in the true light given them by the Holy Spirit who gives true peace to the heart.

As they receive the word of the Lord, old wounds may be remembered and as they find healing and change under the hand of God they may need protection. God's word can set them free but the devil will get in there like greased lightning, if he can, to render the word ineffective and to rob them of salvation (Matthew 13:1–23). The best protection comes from the company of believers hospitable in the Lord, people walking humbly with God and able to keep the faith in all circumstances, willing to persevere and endure patiently with those who are searching but unsure and to encourage those who are struggling. This way God's word takes root. We are all unsure and struggle from time to time, and we need each other in order to hear God efficiently.

When the Holy Spirit brings to mind memories of past events which need to be put right with Him a person can be particularly shaky and vulnerable. Some issues can only be put right with God when it is safe enough to allow all the feelings to come out and to allow all the realisations. Sometimes memories are expressed in your physical body before they can become conscious.

It is quite common for there to be regressive behaviour in which the body automatically behaves as it did long ago, by way of recalling old ways of coping before something or other happened which has never been healed. You may not really be aware of the meaning of your behaviour when this is happening. For example, what memories are, in truth, associated with your habit of curling up into a little ball on the settee and sucking your thumb when you feel stressed? God wants to heal all that! But the healing involves opening it all up to Him, usually with the help of generous people who are willing to give you time and space and whom you respect enough to listen to, so that they can tell you enough of what you are doing, and of their own reactions, for you to begin to make sense of it.

Your feelings and attitudes toward such people may not always be nice. Hopefully, you may recognise that some present feelings and attitudes may come from the past, particularly when people unconsciously remind you of past individuals who were significant for you. Because feelings and attitudes are often transferred from the past onto the present this phenomenon is called "transference". The name helps people to have patience and wisdom with difficult behaviour that is not totally appropriate. Sometimes it takes a long time to come into sufficient awareness of the meaning of your behaviour to be truly accountable before God. Meanwhile a lot of people may have been trying to tell you what they think. It is worth taking other people's criticisms seriously because you can learn from them. That is not to say that they are always right, but the Holy Spirit can tell you the truth about what they are perceiving

about you, and this will help you to know what to take to God
and how to deal with it.

Confusion may be cleared up more efficiently by keeping
regular appointments with some elder who is willing to be
present for you and is able to withstand all you need to sort out.
The Holy Spirit will be working (if invited) to bring what needs
to be dealt with into your mind when you meet. Then it is necessary to speak freely about what comes up, and not censor it.

Embarrassment and shame and fear of rejection can stop
you bringing out into the light all that has to be healed. But if
you can find other people who are able to allow themselves to
be vulnerable and wear their hearts on their sleeves you feel
more able to be vulnerable and wear your own heart on your
sleeve yourself. Thus, when people who have been through their
own healing have come into a place of Godly authority and
anointing in a church it becomes a safer place.

If people imagine that what I have written about in this book
does not apply to them they are living in denial. Everyone in
this world is contaminated by sin. The sin of each one of us is
utterly appalling and far too much for any human agency to
heal. God's church is to be a place of cleansing and repentance
as well as worship (Matthew 11:28–30). The message of Jesus is
a message of salvation for all people here and now and for all
eternity. So we start with the truth of the present and we start
with the mess in the church and we invite in all those who seek
Jesus for healing to share our hospitality and take God at His
word.

Therefore in the true church it will be both safe and necessary to be vulnerable (Mark 14:1–9) although, since strangers
may come in to public meetings, different times and places will
be needed for more intimate fellowship and ministry.
Consequently leaders need to be shrewd enough to treat sin in
the same way God does, to prevent gossip (see 1 Corinthians
6:1–11) and to gain the trust of civic authorities to prevent
harmful misunderstandings (1 Timothy 3:7).

Process

To follow Jesus is to grow closer to Him as time goes on. It involves a lifetime's process of discipleship and change, of healing and maturing. Although in this world we may not achieve perfection in spirit, soul or body, we may press on to take hold of that for which Christ Jesus has taken hold of us, and to be blameless (Philippians 3:12 and 1 Thessalonians 5:23–24).

He heals us not as and when we want it but in order that His kingdom and His glory may be revealed, and we look forward to our resurrection with Jesus and a new heaven and a new earth in which time will be no more (Revelation 10:6) and there will be no more death or mourning or crying or pain (Revelation 21:4). Meanwhile, whilst we are waiting, there is frustration and inward groaning (Romans 8:18–30). Patience is necessary and suffering is to be endured with perseverance (Romans 5:3–5) and with the peace of God (John 16:33) as the world around us gets worse.

Through the Holy Spirit living in them, Christians often find they have compassion and understanding for the practical and political difficulties which beset mankind. For centuries disciples of the Lord Jesus, protected by the institutionalised church, have been of great use to the world by providing people of intelligence and integrity to serve administrations and do good works. Many hospitals and schools began with a Christian ethos. Christianity has kept the peace to a remarkable extent in many parts of the world and Christian social service has served to make Christianity respected in many countries.

Since the two world wars, however, health and social welfare have become increasingly secular. As the influence of the true kingdom church of believers baptised in the Holy Spirit is withdrawn from politics, from academic insitutions and from welfare agencies, and from institutionalised churches too, so a rising tide of legalism, meaninglessness and rebellious lawlessness will shake the world (note 2 Thessalonians 2). If people are to have the opportunity to discover what makes real sense for the sake of true peace and healing, the people who belong to the kingdom of Jesus must not stop meeting together in hospitable community led by the Holy Spirit. Out of our own healing others will find salvation. If Jesus is to be found among us and healing is to take place and real salvation be known, churches need to be real communities where His Spirit is manifest. Hebrews 10:19–25 and 13:1–2, 16 refer to this.

For Jesus to live and reveal Himself amongst us, our relationships need to be right with God so that we meet each other in truth and respond to each other with love. Real community can only develop amongst Christians as a result of our coming individually to the cross of Jesus and receiving our personal healing with heartfelt thankfulness for the price He paid. The necessary submission to God and to one another, without judgement, can only be produced through true and deep personal repentance, so that each person really knows what is owed to Jesus.

The community made up of such people should never advertise itself with any sort of spin or clever advertising psychology. It will be real and true so that Jesus is revealed. Nor does it need to be centred in any particular building, which can so easily become a burdensome expense and an sign of institutionalisation. It can easily be a community of folk who have moved beyond this world's values, living in their own homes and united by their love of Jesus, hospitable and meeting together here and there as led by His Spirit, with respected elders and diverse gifts.

Such a community will generate work to some extent amongst its members and will be able to care for those who belong but are unable to work. A network of mutual support and encouragement will grow from generous hearts not subject to the judgements of this world (1 Corinthians 2:15). Out of weakness and suffering the power and wisdom of God will be revealed (Matthew 5:3–16 and 2 Corinthians 12:9). When the

Spirit so indicates, and when there is faith, believers with appropriate gifts may minister healing with authority in the name of Jesus, sometimes by anointing with oil and sometimes by the laying on of hands (see James 5:14–15).

The light of such a community will become apparent to those in whom God is moving. After all, new wineskins are needed for new wine (Matthew 9:16–17) and the type of real community or church generated through the faithful must not be dictated by the powers of this world. Then, in the midst of increasing secular lawlessness, all sorts of people, both good and bad from streets and country lanes (Matthew 22:10, Luke 14:23), may find salvation amongst us.

POSTSCRIPT

There was a woman who really loved Jesus with a love that affected and blessed many other people. She had met Jesus after she had given birth to her only child, when she was aged 30. Two of the leaders in a local church had spent a lot of time listening to her and praying with her. She was walking in repentance and faith and her nature was changing. Jesus was being reflected in her life for all to see. She had found the peace and joy that only Jesus can bring and, because of her, other people wanted to know Jesus too.

The father of her son was married to someone else. She dwelt in two rented rooms and had scarcely enough money to pay her way because she had had to relinquish her job in order to care for her child. Not long after giving her life to Jesus she developed a cancer in one of her lungs.

The disease did not respond much to the treatment given at the local hospital. It grew and spread rapidly and sapped her strength. She died peacefully within two years of the diagnosis.

Another family in her church had been including her son in many of their activities and when she died they were able to adopt him. Although he was only four, by the grace of God he had seemed to understand quite well what was going on. He had been present when his mother had died and gone to be with Jesus. He joined in the funeral. Thanks and joy were expressed, as well as grief. He has been able to talk about it and to be real about it all in his own way. He is now growing up without too many problems.

God is with us in this imperfect world and He will never leave us (Matthew 28:20). His love for us endures for ever. He knows our infirmities, and will take them in hand, and He will carry all our sorrows for us (Isaiah 53:4) and change us, if we let Him, so that we may reflect His image, and His love, more perfectly here where He has placed us. Perfect healing, however, perfection as this world sees it, is most certainly not a precondition for eternal salvation.

Most of us have to live with aspects of our souls and bodies that are not fully healed. Christ may be formed in us (Galatians 4:19) without every aspect of our bodies and souls being made perfect as this world sees it. Imperfect physical and physiological details are to be overcome practically (Matthew 5:29–30). Weaknesses of the soul are to be overcome by reconciliation with God, by deliverance, and by maturing in character and changing lifestyle, so that we may walk humbly with God and do His will.

Healing does not happen on demand. It does not happen in a way that is within our control. All we can do is clear away, in the time He gives us and under the guidance of the Holy Spirit, all that seems to get in His way, and then seek His face. We depend on His grace and mercy. However, we may as well endeavour to become as aware as possible of the true meaning of whatever we may be suffering so that we may always walk humbly with Him in true repentance and faith, and avoid being deceived. If our ignorance and blindness about ourselves and about what is going on should unintentionally cause us to present our predicaments to God untruthfully, God will not be mocked (Galatians 6:17). He will gently reveal what needs to be apparent to those humble enough to seek Him and He will carry all the pain and embarrassment which may accompany the revelation. He will heal the emotion of it. However, when we are proud, out to win, out to put on a good face, out to overcome in our own strength, in the strength and power of the sciences of this world, or in the strength and power of any spirit other than that of the one true God, we are not humble, not numbered amongst the meek, and liable to go astray and we may fail to receive what He has for us. If we see in His way we shall follow Him better.

It helps to live amongst other people who live in truth and love. Where church is a true community led by the Holy Spirit, healing will take place. True community is therapeutic.

Moses (Deuteronomy 30) Solomon (2 Chronicles 7:14) Micah (6) John the Baptist (Luke 3:3–8) and Jesus (Mark 1:15, Matthew 21:32) all tell us to walk in repentance. Repentance is not about guilt. Jesus takes our guilt. Repentance is a gift from God to help us get right. It involves allowing the indwelling presence of the Holy Spirit to teach us about our own bodies and souls and communities and societies. No matter how badly we have gone astray, both individuals and groups may be reconciled to God and healed through Jesus, His Son, who died for our sin and rose from the dead the third day.

"Therefore we do not lose heart. Though outwardly we are wasting away, yet inwardly we are being renewed day by day" (2 Corinthians 4:16).

PRAYER OF COMMITMENT

Almighty God, creator of all things,
I am thanking you for the free gift of your only begotten Son,
Jesus Christ of Nazareth,
who was crucified on a cross
and died to redeem all sinners,
including me,
who paid the price with His blood
for the sin of this whole fallen world
and rose from the dead on the third day.
I acknowledge my personal sinfulness before you
and come before you in the name of Jesus
for mercy and forgiveness.
You know all things and you know my heart.
I accept Jesus as my saviour.
From now on He is lord in my heart and king of my life.
Please bestow your Holy Spirit to enable me to overcome
this world and my human nature and the devil,
and to change me and heal me and transform my life
so that I may become more like Jesus,
so that I may become your child and follow and obey my king,
and so that He may lead me into eternal life with you.

PRAYER FOR HEALING

This should only be prayed after having prayed the previous prayer, the Prayer of Commitment, from your heart.

Almighty God my Father, I thank you for your promises,
    for your everlasting love and for your faithfulness,
    which endure for ever.
I thank you for sending your only begotten Son, my Lord
    Jesus Christ, to shed His blood to save me.
I thank you for your gift of the Holy Spirit to make me a new
    creation.
You are holy and through the blood of Jesus I am coming
    into your presence.
I seek to be closer to you and to be changed by the power
    of your presence and to be made holy.
I forgive the people who have sinned against me,
    particularly . . .
I confess these sins to you . . . and I renounce them in the
    name of Jesus.
I accept your forgiveness.
By the blood of Jesus I am justified, made righteous, just
    as if I had never sinned.

Fill me with your Spirit and heal me. Please heal . . .
Thank you for your healing.
Please continue to restore my body and my soul.
Heal me day by day.
Continue to change me to be more like you.
Continue to deliver me and set me free in the name of
   Jesus, King of kings and Lord of lords.
Thank you, Lord. Amen!

SELECTED BIBLIOGRAPHY

Secular books are included here because subjects they cover have been neglected by the church for several centuries and handed over to secular agencies. I believe the hand of God is to be found in all the books listed here (as in John 6:44 and 65). They are representative of the way I have been led personally. However, this should not be taken to imply that I agree with everything written in them. Furthermore, I have no doubt that other Christians will be able vastly to enhance my message from their own pilgrimages.

Arnold, E. (1925) *Why we live in Community*. Farmington, PA 15437, USA: Plough Publishing House. ISBN 0-87486-068-7.

Balint, M. (1957) *The Doctor, His Patient and the Illness*. London: Pitman.

Basham, D. (1972) *Deliver Us From Evil*. Grand Rapids: Chosen Books. ISBN 0-8007-9069-3.

Billheimer, P.E. (1977) *Don't Waste Your Sorrows*. Fort Washington: Christian Literature Crusade Inc. ISBN 0-90028-453-6.

Bramhall, C. (2005) *Am I a Good Girl Yet?*, Oxford: Monarch Books. ISBN 1-85424-724-7.

The Book of Common Prayer, The Order for the Visitation of the Sick, and the Communion of the Sick.

Bowlby, J. (1988) *A Secure Base*. London: Routledge. ISBN 0-415-00640-6.

Broadbent, E.H. (1931) *The Pilgrim Church*. Basingstoke: Pickering and Inglis Ltd. ISBN 0-7208-0677-1.

Buber, M. (1970) *I and Thou*. Third edition. English translation by Walter Kaufman. Edinburgh: T. & T. Clark. ISBN 0-567-22338-8.

Chambers, O. (1927) *My Utmost For His Highest*. Newton Abbot: Nova Publishing Ltd. ISBN 0-906330-18-1.

Cox, M. (1988) *Structuring the Therapeutic Process*. London and Bristol, Pennsylvania: Jessica Kingsley, Publishers. ISBN 1-85302-028-1.

Endicott, M. (2003) *The Passion to Heal*. Bradford-on-Avon: Terra Nova Publications. ISBN 1-901949-24-9.

Foucault, M. (1967) *Madness and Civilisation*. London: Tavistock Publications.

Groddeck, G. (1977) *The Meaning of Illness: Selected Psychoanalytic Writings*. London: Hogarth Press.

Hammond, F. & I.M. (1973) *Pigs in the Parlour*. Kirkwood, Missouri: Impact Books, Inc.

Horrobin, P. (1994 & 1995) *Healing Through Deliverance*. 2 Vols. Tonbridge: Sovereign World. ISBNs 1-85240-052-8 & 1-85240-039-0.

Illich, I. (1975) *Medical Nemesis*. London: Calder & Boyars Ltd. ISBN 0-7145-1096-3.

Laing, R.D. (1960) *The Divided Self*. London: Tavistock Publications Ltd. ISBN 0-1402-0734-1.

Laing, R.D. (1961) *Self and Others*. London: Tavistock Publications Ltd. ISBN 0-1402-1376-7.

Laing, R.D. and Esterson, A. (1964) *Sanity, Madness and the Family*. London: Tavistock Publications Ltd. ISBN 0-14-013466-2.

Lynch, J.J. (1977) *The Broken Heart*. New York: Basic Books, Inc. ISBN 0-465-00771-6.

Maycock, A.L. (1938) *Nicholas Ferrar of Little Gidding*. London: SPCK; republished (1980) Grand Rapids, Michigan: William B. Eerdmans Company. ISBN 0-8028-1853-6.

Prince, D. (1990) *Blessing or Curse, You can Choose!* Baldock: Derek Prince Ministries. ISBN 1-901144-02-X.

Prince, D. (1993) *Foundations For Righteous Living*. Baldock: Derek Prince Ministries. ISBN 0-85009-668-5.

Prince, D. (1998) *They Shall Expel Demons*. Baldock: Derek Prince Ministries. ISBN 1-901144-06-2.

Sargant, W. (1957) *Battle for the Mind*. London: Wm. Heinemann Ltd.

Saxby, T.J. (1987) *Pilgrims of a Common Life*. Scottdale, Pennsylvania: Herald Press. ISBN 0-8361-3426-5.

Stacey, J. (2004) *Schizophrenia Defeated*. Bromsgrove: Crossbridge Books. ISBN 0-9543573-4-5.

Tournier, P. (1954) *A Doctor's Casebook in the Light of the Bible*. London: SCM Press Ltd.

Vanier, J. (1979) *Community and Growth*. London: Darton, Longman and Todd Ltd. ISBN 0-232-51450-X.

Vanier, J. (1992) *From Brokenness to Community*. New York: Paulist Press. ISBN 0-8091-3341-5.

Winnicott, D.W. (1986) *Home Is Where We Start From*. London: Penguin Books Ltd. ISBN 0-14-013563-4.

Yonggi Cho, P. (1979) *The Fourth Dimension*. Plainfield, New Jersey: Logos International. ISBN 0-88270-380-3.